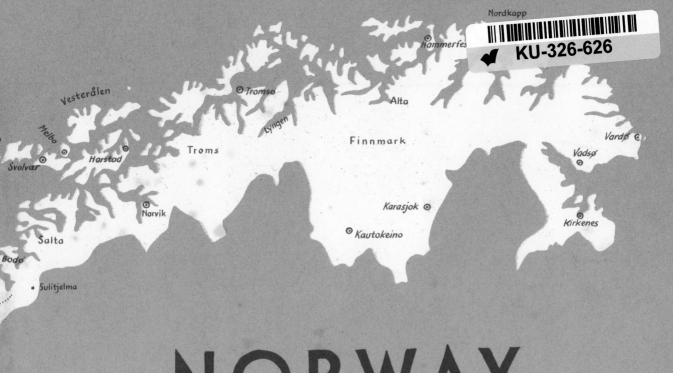

NORWAY

With all good Wishes

H. M. KING HAAKON VII.

From a painting by Agnes Hiorth

NORWAY TO-DAY

*Scenery and Natural Resources · People
and History · Literature, Art and Science
Travel, Sport and Exploration · Economic
Life · Regional Descriptions*

DREYERS FORLAG

OSLO

*Translated into English by
Mai Sewell Fürst and Finn R. Kerr.
Layout: Kjell Dahl.
End papers by Constance Ranheimsæter.*

The photographs have been contributed by

Abels Kunstforlag (Page 64, 86). Aftenposten (84). Aktuell (80).
All-Foto (31 bottom). Einar Bergsland (61 bottom, 65 bottom).
Olav Lorck Eidem (50, 68 bottom, 69 bottom, 70 bottom, 76 top,
78, 79, 87, 90, 99, 104, 106 (both). Alf Endsjø (127, bottom). Norsk
Folkemuseum (19 top, 20 top). J. Chr. Geelmuyden (144, 148 top).
Henriksen & Steen (42, 61 top, 63, 67, 69 top, 72, 73, 75, 103 top,
105, 108, 123, 142, 146). Thor Heyerdahl (57 bottom). Lystad (6, 8,
25 bottom, 58, 74 top, 77, 91, 97, 101, 129, 138). Martelhoff, Amsterdam (83). Elisabeth Meyer (16, 21, 26 top, 52, 62, 109, 110 middle,
117, 119, 122 (both), 125, 126, 143, 149). Mittet & Co. (4, 14, 54, 93,
110 top, 116, 132, 140, 150 top, 152, 153). R. Mørk (26 bottom,
59 top, 60, 70 top, 113, 158 (both). O. Nagell Nicolaysen (5, 10
(both), 147 bottom). Ragnar Anker Nilsen (25 top). Carl Normann
(23, 68 top, 82, 94, 110 bottom (both), 111, 112 top, 120, 127 top, 130
top, 131, 134, 145, 148 bottom, 159, 160). Norsk Telegrambyrås Bil-
led- og Klisjeavdeling A/S (65 top, 71 bottom, 114). Eberh. B.
Oppi A/S (66 top). Polyfoto (48). P. A. Røstad (139). Spies, Amsterdam (85). Ernst Schwitters (18, 27 bottom, 102). Sturlasons
Pressebyrå (27 top, 49, 81). Karl Teigen 15, 17 (both), 19 bottom,
22, 28, 29 (both), 31 top (both), 38). Tore Breda Thoresen (39,
115 top). Leif Tvedt (59 bottom, 71 top, 95, 98, 136, 147 top). Uni-
versitetets Oldsakssamling (12, 20 bottom). O. Væring (9, 13, 30,
32—37 incl., 40, 41, 43, 44 (both), 46, 47, 55, 56 top). O. Dan. Weber
(96). Harald Weedon (24, 103 bottom). Widerøes Flyselskap (154).
A. B. Wilse (56 bottom, 57 top, 88, 89, 100 (both), 118, 124 (both),
128, 130 bottom, 133, 135, 150 bottom, 155, 156, 157). Håkon Sv.
Øyreskleiv (7, 66 bottom, 137, 141, 151).

Contents

EDITOR: PER VOGT

Selection of illustrations: Ragnhild Butenschøn.

A typical valley of Eastern Norway, the Gudbrandsdal.

THE COUNTRY
and Natural Resources.

IN THE EXTREME north-west corner of Europe lies Norway, long and narrow, bounded by the sea on the south, west and north, and by Sweden, Finland and the Soviet Union on the east. From Lindesnes, its southernmost point, to North Cape, its most northerly, it covers more than 13 degrees of latitude, from 57° 59' to 71° 11' N., a distance of 1,750 km. in a direct line. In no other country in the world do civilized people live so near the North Pole.

Although Norways lies, so to speak, on the outskirts of the inhabited regions of the world, she has always been in close touch with the countries beyond her borders, looking seawards, to the west and the south.

Because of her great length and her geographical position, Norway's climate and surface vary considerably: from a friendly, fertile countryside to wild highland plains, snow-covered mountains, forest-clad hills and deep narrow fjords.

Norway, with an area of 324,000 sq.km. is slightly larger than the British Isles. If one includes Svalbard (Spitsbergen and Bear Island), now under Norwegian sovereignty, Norwegian State territory covers about 400,000 sq.km. Only some 4 pct., however, is under cultivation and three-quarters of the country is uncultivable.

Norway may be described as a mountain plateau intersected by valleys and fjords, and only one-fifth of the country lies lower than 150 m above sea-level. Apart from the narrow strip along the coast, the lowlands are found mainly in the south-east and around the Trondheimsfjord. Streching between the valleys and fjords are the so-called "vidda", the undulating highland plateaus covered by typical alpine vegetation and studded with numerous well-stocked fishing lakes. Of these highland plains, Hardangervidda, with an area of abut 12,000 sq.km., is the highest and largest. Rising from these highland plains, for the most part in groups, are mountain summits crowned with eternal snow, the highest lying to the east of the innermost arms of the Sognefjord. Belonging to the mighty group known as the Jotunheimen is Galdhøpiggen, with a height of 2,469 m (8,090 feet),

4

the highest peak in Europe north of the Alps. In all, 26 of the Jotunheimen summits exceed 2,000 metres. After the mountain regions, the forests occupy the largest part of the country (about one-fifth). The most extensive tracts of the uninterrupted forest are found in the lowlands of the south-east and in the neighbourhood of the Trondheimsfjord. The districts bordering the south and west coasts are sparsely wooded, as is the southern part of North Norway. The extreme North is nearly treeless.

Generally speaking, the Norwegian coast falls abruptly into the sea and is repeatedly broken by fjords. The west coast, from Stavanger northwards, is a typical "fjord coastline", very similar to that found in Scotland and Greenland and it is here that the largest fjords in Norway, including the Sognefjord (180 km. i. e. 110 miles), are to be found.

A characteristic feature of this type of coastline is the so-called "skjærgård" (skerries)—a mass of islands and rock formations scattered along practically the entire length of the coast and numbering over 150,000 in all. "The skerries" render navigation to and from the open sea very difficult and dangerous, but on the other hand they offer numerous first-class anchorage and form an excellent inner fairway for coastal traffic.

Equally characteristic of the country are the valleys. In the east they are usually long, comparatively broad, and shallow whereas in the west they are shorter, narrower and deeper. A peculiarity is their irregular or uneven longitudinal profile. Sloping hillsides with swift-running streams alternate with more level stretches with lakes lying in the valleys. The area covered by the valleys is small in comparison with that of the mountain country and such level tracts as occur may be regarded as clefts between the mountains.

Although three-quarters of the country is uncultivable and only a very small percentage of the land area is under cultivation, agriculture, forestry and cattle-breeding have formed the principal occupations of the people from time immemorial. Even in our own days, with its industrial development and growing cities, these pursuits still support one-third of the population. The soil is rich and when tilled gives a good return, a fact which accounts for the remarkably high number of new holdings, mostly small, created during recent years.

On the whole, Norway is far from poor in natural resources. The country possesses many valuable raw materials and an abundant supply of water power.

In the higher regions and in the more northerly parts of the country, cattle-breeding is the most important branch of agriculture. But no less important to the farmer are the forests, and in many parts of the country a farm without woodland is not considered an adequate basis for existence, for the peasant derives a substantial part of his income from this source. Nearly 70 pct. of the forest land is privately owned.

Timber has allways been one of Norways most valuable raw products and, ever since the Middle Ages, one of her most important exports.

To-day, however, wood-products are, for the most part, exported in a highly refined state, and pulp and paper now constitute one of Norway's leading export industries. More than 7 million hectares are covered by forest, 70 pct. of which is coniferous and 30 pct. foliferous. In the most heavily wooded eastern part of the country, the tree-line rises to 900 metres, falling considerably as one moves west and northward. The largest paper and pulp plants are consequently to be found along the rivers, generally near the coast to facilitate shipping of the products. The longest of the numerous rivers traversing the country, such as the Glomma, which is about 600 km. (375 miles) long, are found in the eastern part of the country.

Because of the geographical structure of the country and the position of the water-shed, the rivers, generally speaking, do not attain this length, and those flowing westward are mostly short and swift, forming impressive waterfalls which represent an enormous amount of energy. The total amount of water power has been estimated at about 14 million h.p., more than possessed by any other

The Vettisfoss in Årdal, Sogn, with a sheer drop of 850 feet.

*The riches of the ocean are brought to the surface —
herring fishery off the Western coast.*

European country. Even the rivers of Eastern Norway
and of Finnmark, which often reach a considerable
length, are usually broken by falls and rapids and are
only navigable for shorter distances, but althoug of little
use for traffic, they are ideal for the floating of timber.

Like all lands once covered by ice, Norway possesses
a wealth of inland lakes, which add greatly to the beauty
of the scenery in all parts of the country. Most of them
are small and, as they are usually extensions of a river, are
elongated in shape. Many are among the deepest in
Europe. The largest is Mjøsa, with an area of about
360 sq.km. and a depth of 443 m.

The climate of the inland districts of East-Norway is
dry, pleasant and invigorating, ideal for delicate people.

On the whole, the Norwegian climate is surprisingly
mild, primarily because of the Gulf-stream and the pre-
vailing south-westerly winds, factors which enable people to lead a civilized life as far north as the coasts of the
Arctic Ocean. The climate of the west coast is typically
marine, and no other country situated on the same latitude can show so high mean temperatures. The weather
may be cloudy and windy, with frequent periods of
heavy rainfalls, but the temperature rarely falls below
freezing point.

From time immemorial deep-sea fishing has been the
main occupation of the coastal population. Fish and fish
products (cod liver oil, canned fish etc.) rank among the

chief exports of the country. In the year 1948, the first-
hand value of the Norwegian deep-sea fisheries reached
a total of 325 million kroner, half of which was drawn
from the herring fisheries alone. A greater quantity of
fish is brought ashore in Norway than in any other
European country, and an ever increasing part of the
catch is being exported fresh, iced or frozen. The canning industry has reached a high standard of quality, and
to-day employs several thousand people. In recent years
a considerable industry based on the production of her-
ring-meal and herring-oil has been developed.

The whaling industry is also of great importance and
is a striking example of how a large-scale export industry
may develop when backed by special skill and enterprise.
Modern Antarctic whaling, initiated by the Norwegians
25 years ago, is carried on by relatively large companies,
concentrated in three cities on the western shores of
the Oslofjord, and the expert gunners and crews, who
also work for the large British companies, are all re-
cruited from that part of the country.

The innate capacity of the Norwegians as sailors may
also be counted among the natural resources of the country, because it forms the foundation of Norway's position as one of the world's foremost seafaring nations. Her
merchant marine, after its enormous losses during World
War II, has regained its pre-war volume of 4.8 million
gross tons by 1949. The contributions of the fleet to the

national income played an important part in giving Norway the comparatively high standard of living which she enjoyed before the war.

Closely linked up with the work of post-war reconstruction is a comprehensive plan for the development of the country's industries and the more intensive utilization of its natural resources.

Norway possesses a rich supply of valuable ores and conditions are favourable for large scale development. With regard to electric refining, important electro-metallurgical industries have been established with the aid of abundant water power, and the above mentioned plan includes, among other projects, the construction of a large iron works in Northern Norway.

Timber logs on a lake in one of the south-eastern valleys.

The barren coasts of Norway, from which prehistoric man wrestled a living.

PEOPLE AND HISTORY

FEW EUROPEAN COUNTRIES possess so homogenous a population as Norway. Two main types may, however, be distinguished in her inhabitants, who belong to the Scandinavian branch of the Teutonic group. The first, usually termed the "long-headed", is characterized by a tall, slight build, a long face with the rear of the head prominent, fair skin and hair, and blue eyes. The second, the "short-headed", has a rounder head, is more squarely built and darker in complexion. These two basic types are greatly but unevenly intermingled.

In the north of the country live the Lapps, a people of Mongolian extraction, who represent, however, no more than 1 pct. of the total population. Another small section of the population is to be found in Finnmark. It is composed of some thousands of Finns (termed *Quains* by the Norwegians) who immigrated into Norway from Finland and now form approximately ½ pct. of the total population of the country.

The average height of the Norwegian people is greater than that of most Europeans and they rank, with the Swedes and the Scots, among the tallest nations in the world. Generally speaking, they are strong and well-built. As in Sweden, the average length of life, according to the 1930 statistics, is 61 years for men and 64 for women.

The population of Norway in 1949 is 3,200,000 and the average number of inhabitants per sq.km. is 10 against an average of 47 for Europe as a whole. No other country, however, has so small a percentage of arable land as Norway and the result has been that two-thirds of her people has turned to the coast and the fjords for their livelihood. The remaining one-third lives in the valleys. The greatest density of population is to be found around Lake Mjøsa and near or along both sides of the Oslofjord. Nearly one-third of the Norwegian people are town-dwellers, and the rural population is not concentrated in villages, as in the majority of European countries, but is scattered, living for the most part on single often isolated farms.

From Viking times, travel and adventure have made a strong appeal to Norwegians. Since 1825, more than 1,000,000 have emigrated to all parts of the world and there are now over 2 million people of direct Norwegian extraction living outside Norway, principally in the U.S.A.

The shores of Norway have been populated ever since

8

the receding ice of the last glacial period left a rugged and barren coastline open to human activity. The earliest settlers were nomadic hunters and fishermen who have left their traces in the form of crude stone implements even on the semi-arctic shores of the extreme north, where conditions of life ten thousand years ago must have been very similar to those found on the coast of Greenland and Northern Canada to-day.

The main stream of immigration probably came from the south. It first spread along the southern and western coast, and then gradually forced its way into the densely wooded valleys of the interior.

By the time the Norwegians entered the field of European history in the *Viking Age*, (750—1050 A. D.), the country must have been fairly well populated for thousands of years, the primitive life of hunters and fishermen having long ago developed into a civilization mainly based on agriculture and cattle farming.

Norwegian history in the strict sense may be dated back to the end of the 9th century A. D., when the numerous small kingdoms were united into one by Harald Haarfagre ("Harald the Fair-haired"), whose line continued to rule the country for nearly 450 years. This period is known as the *Saga Age*, in many respects a unique and brilliant era, during which the name of Norway became known throughout Europe. With the introduction of Christianity, about the year 1000, the Norsemen's relations with the Western World gradually assumed a more peaceful character, and, by the Middle Ages, Norway had become a land of churches and monasteries with townships replacing the ancient market places. Foreign trade developed and the natural riches of the country—fish, furs, timber, etc.—became staple articles of trade, especially coveted by the rising German Hansa.

The extinction of the Haarfagre-line in the year 1319 brought about a union with Sweden and later with Denmark, which led to a fatal break in the political and cultural development of the country. In 1450, Norway became almost entirely dependent upon Denmark, the Lutheran Reformation in the 1530's tightening the bonds between the two countries. It is important to note, however, that during this period of Danish domination, which was to last for 364 years, the nation still maintained its existence as a people with their own customs and traditions. The feudal system never obtained a real foothold in Norway, where the peasant continued to live as a free man on his inherited soil. A marked tendency to stress individualism is still one of the chief characteristics of Norwegian life.

The union with Denmark was dissolved in 1814 as an indirect consequence of the Napoleonic wars, when the Power of the Coalition forced the King of Denmark to cede Norway to the King of Sweden. A national assembly meeting at *Eidsvoll* secured the rights of the people, in the form of a free and democratic Constitution, which was signed on May 17, 1814, and a Norwegian Parliament (the *Storting*) was founded. This Constitution made the enforced union with Sweden primarily a personal union and greatly stimulated national, political

The National Assembly meeting at Eidsvoll in the Spring of 1814 gave Norway her Constitution.

Two Norwegian types —
a shipyard worker and a peasant woman.

and cultural life in Norway. The great revival of national life, both materially and
spiritually, during the 19th century, led
eventually to the dissolution of the union
in 1905, when prince Charles of Denmark
was elected king of Norway as *Haakon VII.*
A new era of complete national independence with full sovereign rights began.
Continuous progress in every field has made
the subsequent years a happy period in the
life of the nation, interrupted only by the
severe trial of the German occupation from
1940 to 1945.

In a post-war speech, referring to the
Bevin Plan, the Foreign Secretary, Mr.
Halvard Lange, expressed Norway's will to
co-operate with the Western World:

"There can be no shadow of doubt that,
geographically, economically, and culturally, we are a part of Western Europe, and
we intend to continue our national existence
as a Western democracy."

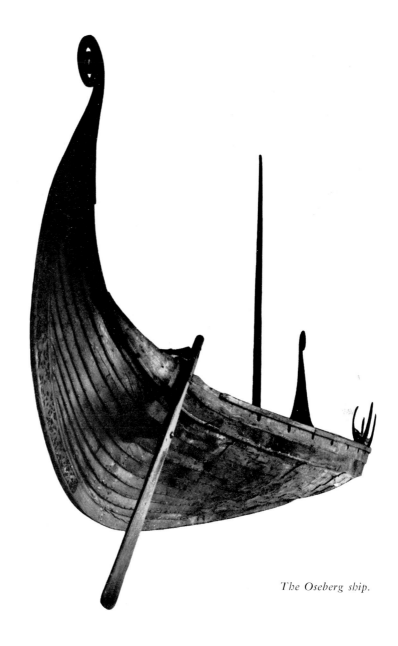

The Oseberg ship.

MONUMENTS OF ANTIQUITY

NORWAY IS the classical home of timber architecture and carving in wood. The Viking ships are among the oldest and finest examples of the genius of Norwegian craftsmen in the treatment of this material, from the point of view of both artistry and technique. The elaborate carving on the prow of the *Oseberg* ship, and the general embellishment and equipment of the vessel, point to an imaginative and artistic achievement which proves that the Vikings in the first half of the 9th century had far higher standards of culture than their plundering of English and French monasteries would indicate at first sight. The staunch and practical construction of the *Gokstad* ship, which belongs to a somewhat later period, is ample explanation of Leif Eirikson's successful crossing of the Atlantic in 999 A. D., some 500 years before Columbus.

Closely related to the peculiar animal-ornamentation of the Viking ships are the dragons and lions that decorate the portals and crown the columns of the so-called "stave"-churches, which represent a method of building in vogue in various Northern European countries during the early Middle Ages.

The method survived longest in Norway, where practically the only specimens extant are preserved. It was in Norway, moreover, probably in the first half of the 12th century, that the method assumed technically and architectonically its most perfect expression. This skeletal construction coincides remarkably in principle

A ceremonial wagon found buried on board the Oseberg ship and dating from the 8th Century A.D.

with that of the Gothic cathedrals. Everything considered, stave-churches, as exemplified by the specimens at Urnes, Borgund and elsewhere, are supreme translations into timber of the Romanesque stone basilicas. Norwegian carpenters also showed their skill in notched timber and log work, a method of construction still employed in dwellings and other buildings requiring warm interiors.

A number of highly characteristic churches, built of notched logs and unpanelled, are still well preserved. Their interiors, with their carved appointments and decorative painting on ceiling and walls, have in many cases been executed with remarkable vigour.

Wainscoting, by no means the least important development in Norwegian timber architecture, is preserved in "Stiftsgården" in Trondheim, now a Royal residence. This is a good example of how the carpenters and woodworkers gave the building a particularly harmonious character by adopting foreign architectural practice.

As the strength of artistic creation was allied so closely to timber architecture, building in stone — which came in with the introduction of Christianity — played

a minor part. Not many relics remain from the early years, but among those still standing mention should be made of the sanctuary of the first saint of the country, St. Sunniva, on the island of Selja. In the inland districts and along the coast, many stone churches of simple construction but of massive and commanding appearance were erected. In the far North, on the border of the territory inhabited by Mongolian tribes, where paganism and witchcraft still prevailed, Trondenes Church still stands with traces of the watch towers built on the churchyard wall as a protection against roving foes.

It is mainly the Romanesque style that characterizes the Norwegian stone churches, but the Gothic style has also left important traces. At the entrance to Jotunheimen, the wild mountain area in the heart of Norway, Dale Church with its richly sculptured portal is an excellent specimen of the Gothic style. Another example, at Stavanger, is the cathedral chancel with its large east window, built after a fire in 1272. The largest and most magnificent piece of Gothic architecture in the country, however, is the Trondheim Cathedral, completed about 1300 in honour of St. Olav, Norway's Patron Saint.

*Elaborate animal carvings adorn the portal of the Urnes stave-church in Sogn,
dating from the latter part of the 11th Century.*

The Borgund stave-church in Lærdal, Sogn.

14

*Norway's patron saint, King Olav, after a wooden sculpture
from Brunlanes, Vestfold.*

Among the notable secular buildings dating from the Middle Ages may be mentioned "Haakonshallen" in Bergen, a large Gothic festival hall built in the period 1247—61; the archbishop's palace at Trondheim, later partly rebuilt, and the fortress of Akershus at Oslo, which was built about 1300 and afterwards became a Royal residence to which many additions have been made until it has reached its present pile. Much re-construction work has also been done in recent years. Somewhat earlier, re-building work had also been carried out on the Bergenhus fortress at Bergen, where the impressive Rosenkrantz Tower was erected to control the Hanseatic merchants in the town. Of a later date are the picturesque feudal palaces of Austråt and Rosendal, as well as the large fortresses of Fredriksten and Kongsten facing the Swedish frontier.

A detail from the reconstructed West Front of the Nidaros Cathedral in Trondheim.

Page 17:

Fortress and Royal residence in olden days, Akershus now is the City's festival hall on official occasions.

One of the big reception rooms of the Castle.

A bridal crown, heirloom of a peasant family.

PEASANT ART AND MUSEUMS OF FOLKLORE

THE MAIN strength of Norwegian peasant art derives primarily from mediaeval forms and decoration. This can clearly be seen even in the styles of peasant architecture, e.g. in the proud lines of the "stabbur", a storehouse for provisions, built of wood and resting on pillars. The "stabbur"'s present-day form, particularly in the Setesdal and Telemark districts, differs from its mediaeval counterpart only in small and unessential details.

Furniture and household equipment were also profoundly influenced by mediaeval design until well into the 18th century. This is especially true of the wrought iron work and of the *art of the silversmiths*, whose use of mediaeval form and decoration in the making of clasps and the large bridal crowns has never disappeared although from 1800 onwards it takes second place to simple filigree work.

Of especial importance is the traditional Norwegian *pictorial weaving*. Technically, it is purely mediaeval and from the point of view of composition it is invariably confined to two planes. Depth and perspective, which may be seen in the productions of European weaveries in the 16th/17th centuries, is not found in Norway.

The national costumes, in the form in which they are still worn in many country districts, bear the signs of an age-old tradition, but a distinction must be drawn between "primary" and "secondary" costumes. The "primary" have their roots in the foot-length women's dress-

es of the Bronze Age, which were made of right-angled panels sewn together. These are to be found in Hallingdal, Telemark and Setesdal. The "secondary", which are found in the other parts of the country, are modelled on the later constantly changing European fashions and are far more closely fitted to the figure. A typical example is the black peasant costume of Western Norway, which is a survival of the 17th century Spanish styles.

Wood carving and the painted rose designs, which are fresh, living and impressionistic, are particularly characteristic of peasant art in Norway. In the Valdres district the renaissance style predominates, while elsewhere, especially in Gudbrandsdalen, the luxuriant and flowing acanthus vine, which reached Norway about 1700, practically dominated the 100 years between 1750 and 1850, the great period in Norwegian peasant art. It was not long, however, before the acanthus *motif* was combined with the assymetrical variations of the rococco style, and the combination of these basic elements has produced developments which vary considerably in the country communities, isolated as they are from each other by Nature.

The art of *"rose painting"* is richest in Hallingdal and Telemark and both baroque and rococco elements display in these districts an instinctive delight in colour and ornamentation which is of a high artistic quality.

The *Empire* style, too, has left its mark, but for the most part in decline. Its formal, rectilinear and rigid character marked the beginning of the end of this luxuriant growth. The rising spirit of industrialism did the rest, and the peasant crafts, which were practised on the farms by the men and women during the long dark winter evenings while tales and jests were told around the hearth, faded quietly away in the latter half of the 19th century.

A cupboard of the early 18th century from Numedal.

Nature has divided Norway into numerous small, separate communities which, in the course of time, have undergone a very varied cultural development. In order to present a vivid and characteristic picture of everyday life in the past, a number of museums have been formed, some of which cover the whole range of national culture, while others specialize in the characteristics of a certain region. Common to all these collections, great or small, is the de-

To-day, the peasant arts and crafts in Norway are kept alive artifically, but it must be borne in mind that this would not have been possible without the instinctive delight which the Norwegian people take in vigorous form and colourful decoration.

sire to create an impression of real life, and many of the small local museums consist simply of an old farmstead, left where it has always stood, fully equipped with its old, well-used furniture, its tools and implements of daily use. When you enter one of these old living-rooms,

Altar cloth, representing the Lord's supper, from the church of Søndeled, 1630.

Rose-painted chest from Ål in Hallingdal.

you almost wonder why there is nobody at home, for the farmer's wife seems to have left her spinning-wheel a moment ago. You look into the barn and the woodshed, where the axe is left in one of the big logs, and no explanation is needed to understand how people lived in this place, long ago. No dull glass cases with crumbling objects on display disturb the feeling of being in a *home*.

Of the big museums constructed on this principle, the most important is *Norsk Folkemuseum* at Bygdøy, a lovely peninsula on the outskirts of Oslo. The

creator of this unique collection, Hans Aall, possessed a rare gift of creating atmosphere around and within the old buildings, which were brought together from every part of the country and re-erected in beautiful natural surroundings. The oldest buildings are a chieftain's hall of the Saga period (about 1200) from Numedal, and a stave-church, from about 1100, brought from Gol in Hallingdal. In connexion with the open air museum, permanent museum buildings have been built to house the enormous collections of furniture, household equipment, costumes and objects of art from the Middle

Creation. Detail from the painted ceiling in the stave-church of Ål, now in the collections of the Historical Museum in Oslo.

*Altar piece in carved and painted
woodwork from Lesja,
Gudbrandsdal.*

*Farm houses of mediaeval type from Setesdal,
now at the Norsk Folkemuseum, Bygdøy.*

*A complete farmstead from Gudbrandsdal in the
Maihaugen collections at Lillehammer.*

Guest room of an Østerdal peasant's home, now at the Glomdal Museum at Elverum.

Ages down to our times, which offer the visitor such a wide and absorbing field of study. The trip to the Folkemuseum can be combined with a visit to the most impressive monuments of antiquity to be seen in Oslo, i. e. the Viking ships, which are placed in their own building near by. To complete the impression of Norway's past, back to the earliest times, one should also see the well displayed collections of the Historical Museum and the Museum of applied arts, both in the centre of the city.

Second only to the Folkemuseum are the open air collections at *Maihaugen* in Lillehammer, created by Anders Sandvig. Here the buildings come almost exclusively from the Gudbrandsdal district. They cover a wide range, from the cottager's holding and the manor house in the valley to the mountain farmstead and the crofter's hut from the high plateau. This museum is perhaps even more beautifully situated on a hillside that commands a superb view of Mjøsa, Norway's greatest lake. In the centre of the Museum park, one finds the ancestral *Bjørnstad* estate with its 26 houses, a typical example of the complete, self-contained communities surrounded by a palisade and dating back to the Viking era, when the owner of a farm instinctively thought in terms of defence. A charming part is also the collection of "seters", small wooden cottages used when the farmers

send their livestock to the high mountain pastures after the long winter period. The museum also contains examples of ancient workshops, where skilled goldsmiths, glass-blowers, wheelwrights and others still demonstrate the skill and the techniques of bygone times.

Among the many other interesting local museums of southern Norway, the *Heiberg collections* at Ambla in Sogn must be mentioned for their outstanding collections of ancient agricultural implements and tools. In *Bergen* the small but very attractive *Hanseatic Museum* merits special attention, and in *Tromsø* you will find a complete display of the cultural life of Northern Norway through the ages.

Space does not allow us to mention more than these few examples of local and regional museums, but wherever you go throughout the country you will meet the people's past alongside its present-day life, often mingling into one, because the local museums are meant to be a living centre of the region's cultural life. On the great festival days, such as Constitution Day—the 17th of May, or Olsok, the 31. of July, when Norway's great saint king Olav fell at Stiklestad, in the year 1030, young and old gather here, and the old people tell how they lived and worked in grandfather's day. It is a tale of harship and toil amidst the overwhelming forces of Nature, and an expression of the Norwegian's love for beauty.

23

ARCHITECTURE

THOSE WHO THINK of architecture in terms of great buildings, or entire sections of cities which have preserved their historical character, are likely to find Norway anything but rich from this point of view, One does not have to seek far for the reasons. In the first place, there is the country's modest position in the European commercial system, which has permitted neither the amassing of large private fortunes nor any possibility worth mentioning for the general development of her cities. Secondly, the standard material used in building is wood which has been, and always will be, popular in Norway because the supply is wellnigh inexhaustible and because wooden houses are warm—an important factor in a northern climate. There are, however, disadvantages, for wood does not endure and the danger of fire is ever present. Indeed, most Norwegian towns have at one time or another been completely destroyed by fire, some of them more than once.

There is yet a third reason, perhaps the most interesting of all in that it is closely related to the social structure of the country. Norway has always been a land of free and independent peasants, for although it is true that she once possessed an aristocracy, it had little or no economic influence and was more or less a *primus-inter-pares* system. It is for this reason that there are few castles or great manor houses. On the other hand, Norway has a very highly developed building tradition in general

which may be seen in the various valleys, Gudbrandsdal in particular.

This tradition is the most important element in the history of Norwegian architecture and its main characteristic is the way in which it has developed through the centuries in accordance with the mode of life and the needs of the locality, influenced by the forms and techniques which the use of timber imposes on the builder. The influence of European architectural styles has, of course, also played a part, but it has worked so slowly that the various forms have been able to adapt themselves to the national traditions and conceptions. It is not surprising, therefore, that Norway takes delight in her old peasant homes, for they represent something genuine and unique in the life of the nation. Worthy of special mention is the strength which springs from their simple plans, the methods of construction and the somewhat vivid decorative work so admirably suited to the large dimly-lighted rooms generally found in these dwellings.

With the introduction of saws, driven by waterpower, in the middle of the 18th century, builders began to use ready-cut material to cover the framework of their houses and, to some extent, built completely in this medium —a more economical method which gave far richer opportunities for architectonic treatment. It was natural that the coastal districts, which were poorly wooded, should lead the way in developing this "panel-technique",

An old farmstead still in use in Upper Telemark.

Court-yard of a small farm in Western Norway.

which found different forms of expression in different districts because of local tradition and the greatly varying climatic conditions. That the modern Norwegian architect is at his best when designing detached wooden houses can be traced directly back to the knowledge and experience gained during this period.

It goes without saying that in Norway, as in other countries, the builders of churches have been influential. There are churches dating from Romance and Gothic times which are usually small and plain but have, on occasion, a surprising and individual richness of detail.

The architectonic confusion which hit the whole of Europe during the last century had a particularly powerful effect in Norway, because the transition from the national tradition, which was locally influenced in the highest degree, to the use of modern materials was extremely violent. It may be said that this is one of the reasons why Norwegian architecture shows even today some uncertainty from many points of view—the country is so elongated and local conditions so varying that the amassing of experience is proportionately difficult. It must also be borne in mind that the tra-

25

"Stiftsgården", a patrician town house of the 18th century in Trondheim, now a royal residence.

A typical example of the intimate charm of one of the "white towns" along the Southern coast (Flekkefjord).

dition of professional architecture is somewhat weak in a country where the design of a house is, in many cases, conceived by the owner himself, without the aid of an architect.

The work of reconstruction after World War II has presented Norway with tasks of unknown proportions and has given the individual architect a feeling of economic and cultural responsibility which is a stimulus to the co-operation always necessary in this field. The results already evident bear the marks of this, in spite of the economic considerations which have confined the architects' efforts to very sober limits. In the smaller Norwegian towns wooden houses are predominant, and towns that still have some of the earlier structures of this kind standing convey, with their low, whitepainted walls, an impression of intimacy and tranquillity.

The central sections of the larger towns usually consist of brick or concrete buildings with a surrounding belt of wooden residential homes. Oslo bears the mark of a rapidly growing city. The city planning, however, does not entirely meet the requirements of modern times, and new architectural styles give much of the city a somewhat unfinished look. Around the

The manor house of Skaugum near Oslo, the home of H. R. H. the Crown Prince.

new City Hall a new centre has developed which is dominated by the international modernistic style of architecture.

Bergen, the capital of Western Norway, is more homogenous. Tradition is alive in this city, where many lovely examples of new and old Norwegian urban architecture may be seen. A characteristic feature of Trondheim, Norway's third city, is the earlier, rectilinear wooden architecture which, together with the well-planned streets, gives the city a lovely and dignified appearance. The skyline of the city is dominated by the

Cathedral, the greatest and, artistically speaking, the most important edifice in the country. Reconstruction is still in progress, and Norwegian architects and sculptors are working to restore this magnificent building which was created at the time when the English Gothic reached its peak 800 years ago.

So far as rural housing is concerned, the tendency now is to get away from the exaggeratedly modernistic style in an effort to develop simple but sanitary and labour-saving dwellings in accordance with the requirements and traditions of the locality.

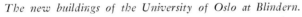

The new buildings of the University of Oslo at Blindern.

APPLIED ARTS
Antiquities.

LET US FOR A MOMENT turn back the clock some 200 years, and imagine ourselves entering the manor house of a distinguished Norwegian civil servant or town merchant. We find ourselves in a room of dignified appearance, with well balanced proportions and a harmonious display of furniture and domestic objects.

We are in the middle of the great century of Norwegian applied arts. This is a cosmopolitan period, and the influence of Continental Europe and, towards the end of the 18th century, England is strong.

The cultural centres are the principal towns. In few other fields are the characteristic features of these centres so clearly evident as in the furniture of the period. The Bergen furniture is slender and graceful, the Trondheim furniture more heavy, while Eastern Norway tends to be richer and more ornamental in design.

Already in the 17th Century Bergen became a cosmopolitan centre under the influence of continental

craftsmen who had fled from war-torn battlefields to settle in this town. Together with their Norwegian colleagues they created a type of baroque furniture adorned with gristle ornamentation. At first the chairs, tables and cupboards reflect the Dutch influence, with their heavy shapes and winding columns, but already about 1660—70 the English influence is apparent. A little later the baroque of Louis XIV gives us the exquisite gilt leather chairs with high backs. This type of chair dominates until the slender, graceful furniture of Queen Anne and George I makes its appearance. The influence of Chippendale's fine art is seen in the work of the late 18th Century.

In a corner of the room there is a fine cast-iron stove, richly adorned with ornamental designs, portraits of the King and Queen, family crests or themes taken from the Bible. Stove-making reached its peak in the 18th Century. The real rococco ornament becomes dominant about 1750, and at the end of the century the stoves look like full-fledged architectural monuments influenced by the antique world.

The most important secular product of the *silversmith* in the 17th Century, is the silver tankard, while the 18th Century brings a great variety of other products, the tea and coffee pot, the chocolate mug and various types of plates and stands. Together with the goblets of the guilds, we find many fine examples of the craftsmanship of the period, which clearly reflects the increasing English influence. The Bergen silver in particular shows great artistic freedom and is of even more exquisite design than that of Trondheim.

Amongst the Norwegian gentleman's most prized possessions we find delftware and glass. Norway had two delftware factories, one of which (Herrebøe) was founded in 1760. The colour of the delftware is blue or manganese, and the craftsmen used a rich variety of themes such as flowers, landscapes and figures on their bowls, plates, tureens, cups and cruet stands. The brush work of the ornaments has a bold touch, as if the master's hand almost casually in a moment of creative inspiration found just the right design or curve with which to adorn his bowl.

Page 28: Cruet stand in blue and white faience from Herrebøe, about 1765.

Glass goblet with cut ornamentation from Nøstetangen, about 1760—70.

Silver tankard from the latter half of the 17th century, made in Bergen.

The Nøstetangen *glassworks*, founded in 1744, was the only factory producing glassware of artistic merit, such as table stands, candle sticks, tankards and elaborate chandeliers. Its finest products, however, were perhaps the exquisite goblets (cups), which were usually made for special occasions. The shapes and cut ornamentation of these goblets call to mind the freshness and creative imagination which characterize the Herrebøe delftware. The themes vary from monograms and coats of arms to allegoric scenes, figural compositions and landscapes. The most striking feature is perhaps the wonderful bluish-violet colour of the glass.

And so we take our leave of the imaginary manor house, with a feeling, perhaps, that the Norwegian gentleman of those bygone days was not so badly off. Luckily, a number of his fine and exquisite treasures may be seen in the museums of applied arts in our principal cities, so why not go and have a look for yourself?

29

Glass flasks with engraved ornamentation by Sverre Pettersen.

Modern applied arts.

DURING THE YEARS preceding World War II, Norwegian applied arts passed through a period of great development and progress. The industry made increasing use of highly qualified designers, and the association "Brukskunst" for the advancement of modern applied arts was founded by interested manufacturers, craftsmen and industrial designers. The assocation secured permanent showrooms in Oslo, and arranged exhibitions all over the country, always striving to improve the artistic taste of the manufacturers and the general public.

When the German occupation ended, it became apparent that the national battle for survival had, in spite of these difficulties, created a generation of first-rate designers with a keen eye for the importance of co-operation. Unfortunately, for reasons of a purely economic nature the industry has been able to make only limited use of the creative vigour and artistic knowledge of these designers.

The supply of raw materials—for which Norwegian applied arts has always had to look abroad—has been greatly reduced since the war because of the lack of foreign currency and the general shortage of such materials. On the other hand, a tremendous need for goods had accumulated during the war. Therefore, in order to achieve the highest possible volume of production, our glassworks and textile factories have had to concentrate on a limited number of products and types.

This makes for a rather paradoxical situation. In spite of a tremendous consumer demand, we have many more designers and new, fully tested models than the industry is able to make use of today. This "seller's market" has tempted some outsiders to sacrifice quality, but this is an exception. Generally speaking, the postwar picture of applied arts in Norway is an encouraging one.

Modern design has taken root and has at the same time found its own national form. There is no antagonism in this. On the contrary, modern design will remain mere jargon until it has gained such a strong foothold in a country that the special national characteristics become an integral part of it. The Norwegian designer expresses himself forcefully, almost dramatically, at the same time utilizing the characteristic features of the various materials in a rather rugged way. The primitive is closer to us than the sophisticated. This is natural in a country where the people are dominated by Nature, where the seasonal contrasts between light summers and dark winters, between warmth and cold, are greater than in almost any other civilized country. The results of these efforts became apparent in a gradual change in the attitude of the public. Modern tendencies and tastes enjoyed a steadily growing interest, while the period-imitation of former days rapidly lost ground.

The German occupation practically stopped all production within the field of applied arts, and it also looked as if it would put an end to the possibilities of theoretical studies and practical training for young craftsmen. The museums were closed down and their collections removed for safekeeping. No foreign books and periodicals were imported, and no Norwegians were allowed to go abroad for studies. The situation looked desperate, but in fact it led to concentration. The will to self-assertion

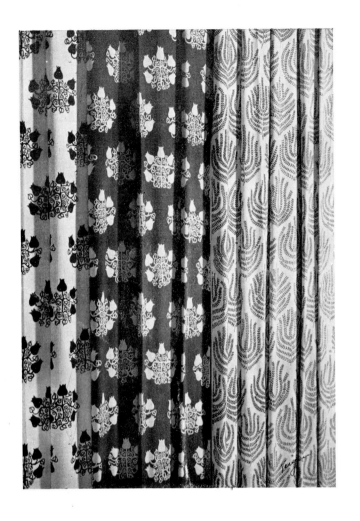

fostered during these years clearly demonstrated that a nation's independence and its national culture are synonymous. Every bombed or burnt-out city was a challenge to the young, the future builders and decorators. Their natural aim was to create some thing better and more beautiful than that which had been lost.

Printed fabrics in modern design from Hjula Væveri.

China bowls from Porsgrunn Porselensfabrikk.

Silver coffee set, designed by Arne Korsmo and made by J. Tostrup.

*Detail from a large mural painting by Henrik Sørensen
in the new Town Hall of Oslo.*

PAINTING

THE HISTORY of Norwegian painting is little more than a century old and it is difficult to point to any marked national characteristic during the first fifty years. The best Norwegian painters went abroad, and lived most of their life outside Norway as Professors at German Academies. It was inevitable that this should set its mark on their art, even though they preferred to choose subjects from their own homeland. It was the German landscape romanticism, that of the Dusseldorf School in particular, which exerted the greatest influence on them.

J. C. Dahl (1788—1857)—who is generally regarded as the founder of Norwegian landscape painting—taught at the Academy in Dresden and won considerable recognition in Germany. His genuine and to some extent realistic appreciation of the element of grandeur in landscape raised his art above the ordinary German romanticism and made it monumental. His unusually sure and living brushwork and a remarkable, shimmering play of colour created an atmosphere and a life in his landscapes which are rarely met elsewhere. Dahl's best Norwegian pupil was *Thomas Fearnley*. His restless nature and wandering life mark his work with a quality at once lively and temperamental which shows

itself to advantage in the few large-scale landscapes he painted.

Another promising and imaginative landscape painter was *August Cappelen*, who died young. There is a dramatic element in his interpretation of the dying forest giants, an atmosphere of dream and of apprehension, which imparts a personal and exciting quality to his romanticism.

It was around *Hans Gude* and *Adolph Tidemand* that the greatest interest gathered in Norway in the middle of the 19th century, in spite of the fact that both were domiciled in Dusseldorf. Hans Gude also achieved a certain importance as a teacher of landscape painting for very many Norwegian painters. Adolph Tidemand, on the other hand, stands in a class by himself as an interpreter of Norwegian peasant life.

For quite a long period (from 1850—1870) the so-called Dusseldorf painters dominated Norwegian art. They completely overshadowed a few Norwegian artists who remained at home and only in the present century achieved their rightful place in the history of Norwegian art. The first of these was *Lars Hertervig* (1830—1902), who developed a remarkable visionary gift for perceiving the play of colour in light and the

Rolf Nesch: The fishing fleet. Nesch is an initiator of modernistic experiments in painting.

painters primarily interested belonged to the Werenskiold group, in the first instance Per Krohg and Axel Revold. Other followed, among them *Alf Rolfsen, Aage Storstein, Reidar Aulie* and Henrik Sørensen. These artists have produced many works on the grand scale, a new and interesting development in Norwegian Art which has attracted much attention abroad.

The decade between 1930 and 1940 has been a fruitful one for the younger element in Norwegian painting from many points of view. The various currents in French art, where imagination and strong logical composition made themselves felt, gave new stimuli to the younger artists who were thereby enabled, without being directly influenced, to cast new light on the art of the older Norwegian painters, including Hertervig, Stoltenberg and, not least, Edvard Munch. *Kai Fjell* and *Arne Ekeland* occupy a particularly prominent place within this generation.

They have a remarkable gift for letting their imagination play on clearly defined ideas expressed in a new, rhythmic style both in composition and colour. Kai Fjell finds expression in a solemn worship of Woman as the unsullied Madonna, and of Nature as the fruitful Mother Earth. Every-

thing in his work, its form and its finely attuned use of colour, is marked by this deference for Woman and her appointed role as mother. Arne Ekeland lets his imagination play over the proletariat's golden future and its battle to reach its goal. There is a renaissance-like power in everything he does. Finally, mention must be made of *Erling Enger*, whose portrayal of life on the family farm and the surrounding Nature has intensity and an incomparable humour.

Kai Fjell: Mother and child.

Per Hurum: Preliminary work in clay for a monument to the victims of the Second World War.

SCULPTURE

Norwegian sculpture did not gain a place in the consciousness of the Norwegian people until about the turn of the century, and then chiefly through the individual achievements of a few outstanding artists rather than of a large group of sculptors. Actually, such a group emerged only about the middle of the 'twenties.

The first Norwegian sculptor to gain the recognition of his people was *Julius Middelthun*, who really left only one monumental work and two busts—the distinguished statue of A. M. Schweigaard in the University Square, Oslo, and the busts of the poets Wergeland and Welhaven. After him, it is especially *Brynjulf Bergslien* of the elder generation who has made himself noted with his equestrian statue of Carl Johan before the Royal Palace.

It is only towards the end of the 'nineties that a sculptor of eminent talent appears, attracting attention through the compelling and forceful nature of his work, his abundance of ideas and his prolific creative production. In the first eight years, *Gustav Vigeland* created several groups dealing with the theme "Man and Woman", and a great number of fine busts of prominent men. He reached the height of his creative energy in what is perhaps his most eminent monumental work, the memorial to Norway's illustrious mathematician Niels Henrik Abel.

About 1908 he showed his first sketch-model for a fountain, which attracted tremendous attention and brought him wide acclaim. The Fountain became his life work to which he consecrated practically all his creative energy, gradually developing the original idea into a great monumental project. The Municipality of Oslo finally approved his plan, and provided him with the necessary means and space to proceed with the work.

However, already at that time, and later as well, warnings were sounded against this ambitious project, but they have fallen on deaf ears and only served to stimulate the artist to expand his plans and to demand ever more space for the sculpture park.

After having considered a number of other sites, suitable space was finally provided in the municipal Frogner Park in Oslo, where in a few years the project will be completed in accordance with the plans of Vigeland, who died in 1943. In its present shape, with the Fountain serving as the centre of a gigantic monumental park and the monolith reaching towards the skies, it is extraordinarily impressive. Like all great conceptions, it inevitably arouses controversy, and final judgement is perhaps better left to later generations.

Gustav Vigeland: Bronze group from the bridge at the Frogner Park in Oslo.

In spite of the enormous amount of work which Vigeland put into this gigantic project, he still found time for a number of other great statues, among them notably one of Henrik Wergeland in Kristiansand, and the lovely statue of Camilla Collett in the park of the Royal Palace in Oslo.

A striking contrast to Vigeland's forceful and expressive, but frequently rough, figuration is the work of *Ingebrigt Vik*. Some of Vik's figures bear evidence of a profound study of the human body, which he has succeeded in translating into a fine and highly sensitive plastic figuration.

The talented *Wilhelm Rasmussen* deserves mention as the sculptor who has perhaps had the greatest influence

Gunnar Janson: The poet Arne Garborg.

Grimdalen also emphasize simplicity of form with strong surface effects in the treatment of the material so as to bring out the character, while Dyre Vaa rather strives to achieve this effect through an exaggeration of the motif of movement, thereby giving life to the figure but sometimes also a feeling of unrest in the plastic form. Per Palle Storm has made profound and exacting studies of the human anatomy, and models his sculpture more on this knowledge than by trying to bring out the statuary form through purely plastic means of expression. He is now a professor at the Academy.

Notable among the second group are *Stinius Fredriksen, Ørnulf Bast, Emil Lie, Nils Flakstad* and *Emma Matthiassen*. These artists seek to combine their impressions of classical sculpture which they have studied abroad, with the knowledge and ideas they have gained from the Norwegian Gothic in the Nidaros Cathedral. They work chiefly with purely plastic means and motives, but nevertheless manage to get something typically Norwegian into the character and form of their sculpture.

Nils Flakstad achieves this effect directly and consciously, the others rather through instinct and intuition. Emil Lie and particularly Stinius Fredriksen emphasize a plastic and well-balanced placidity in the form, and through a sensitive, delicate modelling of the figure they obtain a feeling of latent warmth and inner life in their sculpture. The same effect is also apparent in the work of Emma Mathiassen —mainly finely characterized busts—although in a more unemotional and discreet manner, while in the work of Ørnulf Bast it manifests itself as a robust and healthy sensualism. Per Hurum and Josef Grimeland, both active with sculptural work in connection with the new City Hall in Oslo, may also be mentioned here. Their work rests on the classical tradition, although it is also inspired by modern French sculptors.

After the liberation, when a number of new and very promising young artists emerged, it became apparent that Norwegian sculpture is undobtedly in a period of great progress and development.

on the new generation, partly as an instructor at the Academy of Art and partly for his idea of giving the most promising of his graduate students an opportunity to work on the restoration of the West Front sculpture of the Nidaros Cathedral in Trondheim. These young people emerged in the middle 'twenties as a distinguished group of talented artists, and created what in the real sense of the word can be termed Norwegian sculpture. They have attracted much favorable attention from the other Scandinavian countries.

These artists fall more or less into two groups. The foremost exponents of the first group are *Gunnar Janson, Per Palle Storm, Dyre Vaa* and *Anne Grimdalen*. In general it may be said that their figures are forceful and alive with movement and rhythm. Gunnar Janson and Anne

Ørnulf Bast: The two sisters. Terracotta, preliminary to the monument presented to Denmark as a token of the Norwegian people's gratitude for aid during the Second World War.

Josef Grimeland: The Oslo girl. Decoration for the City Hall of Oslo.

Per Palle Storm: Sitting athlete. (Plaster, later cast in bronze for the National Gallery in Oslo).

41

Ludvig Holberg with two characters from his plays.
Bronze group by Dyre Vaa near the National Theatre in Oslo.

LITERATURE

THE LITERATURE of the Middle Ages was centered around the court and the church. It was the pride of even the viking kings to be surrounded by poets who could praise their deeds and hand them over to posterity. Some of the most eminent literary monuments from the Middle Ages of Norway are these "kvad", many of which are included in the chronicles of the kings—the "sagas", written in Iceland in the 12th and 13th century. They are highly developed works of art, terse and strong in style and with a judicious use of symbols and metaphors. The "sagas" are the main sources of the history of that time, but they are still more novels, exquisite in their descriptions of persons and situations, with a strong sense of humour and with precise and striking dialogue. As contact with the leading European countries grew stronger throughout the Middle Ages, the ballads, novels and hymns of France and England were translated into Norwegian, deeply influencing the artistic and imaginative sense of the people. Many manifestations of this are to be found in popular art throughout the centuries.

The end of the Middle Ages witnessed a catastrophic decline in creative Norwegian literature, and the Renaissance scarcely gave Norwegian literary life any revival

worth noticing. The only writer of 17th century Norway whose work has had a lasting literary value is *Peter Dass*, a clergyman from the north of Norway, who in his "Trumpet of the North" gave lively poetical descriptions of Nature and the people's life.

A classic example of the cultural situation of Norway in the 18th century is *Ludvig Holberg*. He was born in Bergen and went to school there. But as the only university of Denmark-Norway was situated in Copenhagen he went to study there, and never returned to his native country which afforded no facilities for his scientific and dramatic activities. He is the most outstanding personality in the cultural life of the twin-countries in the 18th century. He introduced modern impulses from French and English philosophy and political science. He may also be regarded as the founder of Danish and Norwegian theatre. Partly influenced by Molière he wrote a great number of comedies, of which ten or twelve still belong to the standing repertory of the theatres in both countries.

Toward the end of the 18th century a growing Norwegian self-consciousness heralded the coming separation from Denmark, but is wat not until after 1814 that Norwegian cultural and literary life attained its renaissance. The great name in this new spring-time is *Henrik Wergeland*, still the main central personality in Norwegian literary history. He worked tirelessly, inspired by the ideas of the French revolution and of his own burning genius, his writings varying from popular education to sublime love poetry, from farces to sermons. He died at the age of 37, having in his short lifetime influenced the outlook of his people more deeply than any other Norwegian poet before or since.

The last part of the hectic 19th century is primarily dedicated to the two giants who for the first time called the world's attention to Norwegian literature: *Henrik Ibsen* and *Bjørnstjerne Bjørnson*. The production of these two authors laid a sure foundation for modern Norwegian theatre. Both of them began with plays on national and historical themes, but at the beginning of the 1870's they joined the modern realistic school, giving in their turn vital incentives to European theatre. They were widely different, Ibsen was mainly concerned with the problems of the individual while Bjørnson regarded his task from a broader national point

Henrik Wergeland. Detail from the monument in Kristiansand, by Gustav Vigeland.

of view and with his plays, poems, novels and articles took an active part in political and social life. Together with the brilliant novelists *Alexander L. Kielland* and *Jonas Lie* they form the four cornerstones of modern Norwegian literature.

During the union with Denmark Danish had become the written language of Norway, differing considerably from the language spoken by the people throughout the country, and the national revival brought forth the claim for a written language which might be a more adequate idiom for the people as a whole. About the middle of the 19th century the linguist *Ivar Aasen* created his "landsmål" or "nynorsk" (New Norwegian) language on the basis of the different Norwegian dialects. His work gave birth to a cultural and literary movement counting today some of our most exquisite poets and novelists, among whom should be mentioned *Arne Garborg*, *Olav Aukrust* and *Olav Duun*.

In the Norwegian literature of the 20th century two main streams are discernible. A great number of poets and novelists have dedicated their talent to artistic description of the nature, the popular life and the social development of their native regions, thus giving a very rich and lively picture of the nation's life and mentality. Foremost among these we find *Johan Falkberget*, half poet and half historian in his great novels from the old mining town Røros, and *Johan Bojer*, who has won a great public abroad, while the in many ways profounder but less accessible thinker and poet *Hans E. Kinck* is but little known outside his country.

Others have mainly been occupied by modern intellectual, social and psychological problems, in contact with and partly very much influenced by the contemporary poetry, drama and novel of especially England and America, partly also France. Several of the modern Norwegian authors have won world-wide fame, especially to be mentioned are *Knut Hamsun* and *Sigrid Undset*, both of whom have been awarded the Nobel prize.

After a flowering-period in the 1920'ies the novel has shown a marked decline in latter years, while the sufferings of World War II brought forth a profusion of poetry. Among those who added not only to the nation's

power of resistance during the German occupation, but also to the spiritual treasure of all times must be mentioned *Arnulf Øverland* and *Nordahl Grieg*. The former spent nearly four years in German prisons and concentration camps, while the latter died a hero's death during a bombing flight to Berlin. No doubt the concentration camp diary of *Odd Nansen* will also be counted among the truly great and inspiring human documents of a period now passing into history. It is interesting to note that whereas literary activity almost stopped under the compulsion of Nazi censorship, the habit of reading grew. The novelists and dramatists, essayists and writers of popular scientific works who have enriched the nation's intellectual life enjoyed a popularity previously unknown even in this nation of keen readers.

Henrik Ibsen. Drawing by Erik Werenskiold.

Bjørnstjerne Bjørnson at his farm Aulestad in Gudbrandsdal. Oil painting by Erik Werenskiold.

Olav Aukrust. *Arnulf Øverland.* *Nordahl Grieg.*

Knut Hamsun. *Johan Falkberget.*

Olav Duun. *Sigrid Undset.*

Decorative sculpture by Stinius Fredriksen.

MUSIC

MUSICAL LIFE in Norway in the 18th century was linked with the Music Societies to be found in the larger towns, and special mention must be made of the Bergen Society "Harmonien", established in 1756. Like all the other organisations which encouraged music, however, it devoted the greater part of its attention to foreign works. *Waldemar Thrane* (1790—1828) produced the first important Norwegian composition, his work for voices, "Fjeldeventyret". *Ole Bull* (1810—1880) also wrote compositions which were markedly Norwegian in character, but he is best known as the master violinist around whom so many legends have been spun. We do not find music purely Norwegian in character until the middle of the century, when it grew out of the Romantic movement which reached Norway about 1840. This so-called "national awakening" had its origin in the rediscovery of forgotten or hidden national values. It called forth new powers in Norwegian cultural life and music benefited considerably. The folk tunes which *Ludvig M. Lindeman* (1812—1887) wrote down and preserved showed clearly that, during the 400 years of association with Denmark, there had been created in the country districts a wealth of melody which could give life and energy to the music about to be born. Lindeman was himself an outstanding composer of church music, whose hymns revivified Norwegian church singing.

It is generally recognised that Norwegian folk music, as we know it to-day, is unusually rich, versatile and individual. The many ancient traits preserved in it are due to the influence which medieval church music exerted in Norway. During the 5 centuries for which the Catholic Church held sway (until 1537) Masses echoed throughout the land and the profound impression they made was not easy to eradicate. It can be found for instance in the lullabies and elsewhere, but it is seen most clearly in the style of Norwegian melody, which is so different from that of the other northern countries. The isolation of the country districts was unfortunate politically, but culturally it was an advantage from many points of view.

The composers who drew from this well for their compositions were first that master of romance *Halfdan Kjerulf* (1815—1868) and *Rikard Nordraak* (1842—1864), the composer of Norway's national anthem, who died young. Both are mainly concerned with song and their work is closely linked with the great romance poetry, the works of Welhaven and Bjørnson. The most characteristic composer of all, however, so far as national romantic music is concerned, is *Edvard Grieg* (1843—1907), who is pre-eminently Norwegian in his music, even though he never drew directly from folk music for his inspiration. The boldness of melody which is so typical of Western Norway and, incidentally, is related to the music of Scotland, is markedly characteristic of Grieg's themes, and the influence of the *Hardingfele* is also noticeable in his harmony. Grieg, on his father's side, came of Scottish stock. The works of his great contemporary, *Johan Svendsen* (1840—1911) are entirely different in temper. He came from East Norway and it has been

Rikard Nordraak. Detail from his monument, by Gustav Vigeland.

Edvard Grieg.

said that his symphonies reflect the quiet colours of this part of the country. Svendsen was Norway's greatest orchestral conductor. In 1871 he co-operated with Grieg in founding the Society of Music, which greatly stimulated not only the capital's but the entire country's interest in music. The present Philharmonic Society, which was established in 1919, is a continuation of the earlier organisation.

Modern ideas in Norwegian composition can already be discerned in Svendsen's works, in that his technique is to some extent influenced by the French *esprit*, but it was *Johan Selmer* (1844—1910) who first brought Berlioz's conceptions to Norway. He was, in fact, the champion of programmatic music in the land.

Hjalmar Borgstrøm, (1864—1925) also devoted his attention to this field. Both he and Selmer knew thoroughly how to use the orchestra and the same is true of *Gerhard Schjelderup* (1859—1923), Norway's greatest writer of *Dramatic Music*, who was much influenced by Wagner. The orchestral works of *Christian Sinding* (1856—1941) are also marked by the influence of the German master.

All the composers mentioned have also made their contribution to Norwegian romance and have set Norwegian lyrics to music. Among the romance composers, mention must also be made of *Agathe Backer-Grøndahl* (1847—1907), who has been called the world's greatest woman composer.

From the beginning of the present century, various European influences have made themselves felt, above all Debussy's. From the 1920's onward, however, a reawakened interest in the national music has been perceptible. This indefinable quality, which must be called "national" for want of a better name, is abundantly evident to all Norwegians in the works of *Monrad Johansen* (1888—), *Sparre Olsen*, (1903—), *Eivind Groven* (1901—), *Bjarne Brustad* (1895—) and others. Outstanding writers of symphonies are *Irgens Jensen* (1894—) and *Klaus Egge* (1906—), who bases some of his compositions on the technique of the *Hardingfele*. Orchestral talent is also evident in the works of *Harald Sæverud* (1897—). *Fartein Valen* (1887—) is a solitary figure, who has formed his own atonal mode of expression and has only in recent years won general recognition.

Opera has few exponents in Norway, partly because composers have had only occasional opportunities to present works on the stage. In this category, in addition to Schjelderup, must be mentioned *Ole Olsen* (1850—1927), *Johannes Haarklou* (1847—1925), *Catharinus Elling* (1858—1942) and *Arne Eggen* (1881—).

Norwegian talent in this field has consequently been forced to look to other countries, where it has done well. It will suffice, in this connection, to mention only *Kaja Eide* ("Norena") and *Kirsten Flagstad*.

Norway has many fine artists, pianists in particular, the best known of whom is *Robert Riefling* (1911—).

*"The Death of Aase."
Scene from Ibsens's
"Peer Gynt", with
Hans Jacob Nielsen
in the role of Peer.*

THEATRE

THE HISTORY of dramatic art in Norway is not a long one. Not more than a century ago it existed only in the form of private entertainment stimulated by occasional visits by companies of foreign, mostly Danish, players. A first attempt at national emancipation was made by *Ole Bull*, the famous violinist and art-enthusiast, who, in 1850, founded "Den nationale Scene" in his native city Bergen, where two young men who were later to become the dominating forces in Norway's theatrical life, *Henrik Ibsen* and *Bjørnstjerne Bjørnson*, had their first somewhat bitter experiences as playwrights and producers. But the strong national development of the latter half of the century soon found its natural expression on the stage; Norwegian drama of high class came into being, and a brilliant phalanx of young actors appeared. The theatre became what it has remained ever since: an active center of the nation's cultural life. Under the inspiring leadership of *Bjørn Bjørnson*, the poet's son, the "National Theatre" in Oslo was inaugurated in 1899. By dedicating its efforts first and foremost to performing the masterpieces of Ibsen and Bjørnson in an adequate setting, it soon succeeded in creating a tradition of quality, especially in the field of realistic drama, which may be said to have determined the character of the Norwegian stage up to the present day. Among the younger playwrights of note, *Gunnar Heiberg, Nils Kjær* and *Helge Krog* must be mentioned, while the number of eminent actors whose names are indissolubly connected with the history of the Norwegian stage is too great to be rendered within this brief record.

Theatrical life in Oslo is not, however, limited to one stage only. At present no fewer than eight permanent theatres give performances, ranging from Shakespeare to Sartre and Anouilh, with an ample interlading of light entertainment. Permanent theatres of high standing are also to be found in Bergen, Trondheim and Stavanger, and, as an effective means of bringing dramatic art into the remotest parts of the country, a new institution has been brought to life under the name of "Riksteatret" (The State Theatre). By arranging extensive tours with well-equipped companies, this state-supported organisation brings the theatrical events of the cities within reach of large parts of the population who now for the first time experience the art of the stage. The two leading Oslo theatres, Nationaltheatret and Det Norske Teatret as well as the provincial theatres are supported by the State and the Municipalities.

The events of the War of 1940—1945 and the sombre experiences of the German occupation with its threat of destruction to material and spiritual values alike, are perhaps still too near to find an expression of lasting value in dramatic writing. The contemporary Norwegian theatre suffered a heavy blow through the death of *Nordahl Grieg*, the poet and playwright who was reported missing after a raid on Berlin in 1943. The theatres to-day maintain close contact with modern European and American drama, and among the best performances of the post-war seasons were plays by Maxwell Anderson, Thornton Wilder, Tennessee Williams, Somerset Maugham, Noel Coward, Terence Rattigan and others.

The State Broadcasting House in Oslo, with the new University buildings in the background.

BROADCASTING

THE FIRST NORWEGIAN broadcasting station — a modest 500 Watt transmitter located in Oslo — was heard in February, 1923. A few years later its power was increased, and in December 1929 it was moved to Lamberseter outside Oslo, where it is still operating at 60 KW. Since that time a number of medium strength transmitters have been put into operation in other cities.

Private broadcasting ceased in 1933, when the Norwegian Government Broadcasting Service was established as an independent Government enterprise with exclusive broadcasting rights for Norway. Administratively, the Broadcasting Service comes under the authority of the Ministry of Education, and is headed by a Board of five members appointed by the King.

The managing Director is assisted in an advisory capacity by a Broadcasting Council of fifteen members.

The Norwegian Government Broadcasting Service currently operates 28 long and medium-wave transmitters totalling 357,625 KW, as well as 8 transmitters in the short-wave bands.

The geographical conditions in Norway — the enormous distance from the South to the North, the high mountain ranges, the deep valleys and narrow fjords, as well as the sparsely populated areas in many parts of the country, make it both difficult and costly to bring the national programmes into the homes of all Norwegian listeners. It might be mentioned in this connection that the national hook-up between the various broadcasting stations covers a distance of 4,343 kilometers.

On January 3, 1938, the Norwegian Broadcasting Service inaugurated its special broadcast to Norwegians abroad, to seamen and whalers, and to the great number of residents of Norwegian descent in North America who understand Norwegian.

These programmes take 3½ hours each day. They are broadcast over 8 frequencies in the short-wave bands with a transmission power of 100 KW.

The regular national programme runs into a total broadcasting time of some ten hours per day. In addition to this regular schedule there are a number of local programmes, chiefly reports and news of local interest. Norway is the only country in the world having a regular broadcast in Samian, the language of the Lapps.

The statistics show that 73 per cent of the national programmes originate in the national broadcasting studios in Oslo, while 25 per cent are transmitted from the local stations.

In Oslo, the Norwegian Broadcasting Service is housed in a modern building with up-to-date studio and office facilities. All the latest technical innovations and equipment in radio have been taken into use.

As of May 24, 1949, there were some 688.000 licenced listeners or approximately 215 listeners per 1000 inhabitants. In proportion to total population, this puts Norway in sixth place in Europe, and the number is increasing steadily. There is a licencing fee of kr. 20 per year (£ 1) to use a receiving set. In addition, the Norwegian Broadcasting Service places special tax on new receiving sets. These revenues make the Norwegian Broadcasting Service a self-supporting institution.

The primary mission of the Norwegian Government Broadcasting Service is to bring enlightenment and education to the people, to be a dependable source of news and information and to provide good entertainment.

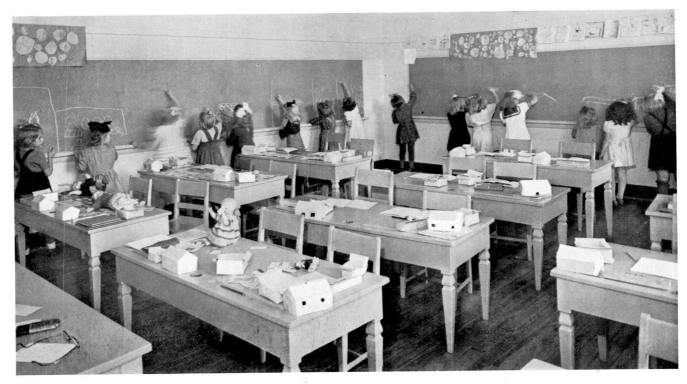

Classroom in one of the elementary schools of Oslo.

EDUCATION

MOST NORWEGIANS are perhaps somewhat inclined to overrate the quality of the school system of their country. This may be a consequence of the rapid growth and expansion of the Norwegian schools during the second half of the 19th century, and the resulting relatively high educational standard of the country.

Since that time the framework and organizational set-up of the school system have undergone some changes, but the quality and standard of the schools have continued to grow. Compulsory schooling (elementary schools) is still 7 years (from 7 to 14 years of age), but today these years are used to much better advantage than previously.

The *elementary schools* (folkeskolen) are run by the local municipalities, and tuition is free. Very few pupils attend private schools. The heir apparent, Prince Harald, for instance, attends a regular elementary school. Owing to the sparseness of population in some parts of the country, many schools are quite small. During the school year 1948/49, nearly 7,000 children (3 per cent of all school children) attended so-called *"undivided"* schools, i. e. schools in which 6 to 12 pupils are taught together in the same class, regardless of sex and age.

In the School Act of 1936, practical subjects were given a more prominent place in the school plan, and manual and physical training became compulsory. Where

conditions permit — particularly in the urban elementary schools — *English* is taught during the last two years in addition to the regular subjects.

Good progress was being made before World War II in the work of securing school buildings that satisfied pedagogic and sanitary requirements; today, however, much is lacking in this respect. During the next 10 years, a very great number of new schools will have to be built.

The most recent educational plans, which in part are based on scientific pedagogical research, have prepared the way for a more effective and liberal method of teaching. The general tendency is to encourage the initiative of the pupils and their ability to work independently, to provide an outlet for their artistic inclinations and creative urge, and to further group work and social activities.

A feature which is characteristic of Norwegian schools is that *all* advanced education is based on the elementary school. This unified school system was forced through by radical school politicians, who maintained that in a sparsely populated country it was an advantage for the children to remain at home as long as possible, and that it gave added strength and substance to the elementary schools when the pupils were able to continue in the same class together for a period of seven years. Moreover, an elementary school for *all* children would be a *real* elementary school.

The elementary school forms the basis of a varied system of advanced schools. Directly connected with the elementary schools are the so-called *continuation schools* (framhalsskoler), which were established by the School Act of 1946. These schools give courses of one or more years' duration in general subjects, and there is some opportunity for specialized training in certain practical subjects, which are suited to local requirements, e. g. courses in fishing, farming etc.

If a municipality should so decide, the continuation schools may be made compulsory for pupils who do not wish to attend other advanced schools.

For young people over 17 years of age, particularly in the rural districts, there are special *"youth schools"* (ungdomsskoler), 6-months boarding schools that teach subjects of a more theoretical nature than those taught at the continuation schools. These schools — among them the so-called "people's high schools" — are frequently of a strongly national or religious character.

Then there are the various *trade schools* (Act of 1940), technical schools based on the elementary school. The pupils attend these schools before, during and after their apprenticeships in industry and handicraft. There are, furthermore, a great number of ordinary vocational schools.

As already mentioned, *the secondary school* (Act of 1935) is based on the elementary school. It falls into two parts: The *"realskole"*, which is usually of a 3-year duration, and the *"gymnas"* (high school), which usually takes 5 years. For the first two years, identical subjects are taught in both schools. After two years the pupils have to decide whether they wish to continue for one more year, taking the *"realskole" examination* which qualifies for subordinate positions in trade and commerce and in various departments of the public services (post office, telegraph office, customs, railway etc.), and for entrance to commercial schools, technical schools etc., or whether to continue for another three years, taking the *matriculation examination* ("examen artium"), which qualifies for advanced studies at the Universities.

The major subjects taught in the "realskole" are Norwegian, English, German, arithmetic and mathematics. The "gymnas" has several different "lines". Nearly half of the pupils attend the "English" line, majoring in Norwegian and English, and an almost equal number attend the so-called "Science" line, majoring in Norwegian, mathematics and physics. The other lines — "Latin", "Old Norse" and "Russian" — attract relatively few pupils. A new line — the "Natural Science" line — teaches less mathematics, but more chemistry and biology than the "Science" line. French, English and German are taught in all lines.

What has been said about the teaching methods in the elementary school also applies largely to the secondary school. The educational work stresses the *class*, not the individual pupil as a unit. It is rigidly confined to the teaching of fixed subjects, to plans and examinations, and is primarily based on the imparting of knowledge and the development of skills and proficiency. However, the School Act leaves considerable scope for radical educational experimentation, and plans have already been drawn up which — when fully realized — will encourage the individual activity of the pupils and appeal to their initiative to a much greater degree than previously.

A peculiar feature of the secondary school in Norway is the extraordinarily high number of pupils who take the matriculation examination ("examen artium"). In 1947 the number was 5,272 as against 4,236 in Sweden and 2,945 in Denmark. The figures per 1,000 inhabitants are 17, 6.2 and 7.2 respectively. The increase has been especially heavy since 1940.

In contrast to so many other countries, therefore, there is no real shortage in Norway of students seeking a higher academic education. Indeed, in some fields the number of applicants for the University and the College is so great that a qualitative selection has to be made, usually on the strength of marks attained in the matriculation examination.

For trade school teachers a special teachers' college has been established, and the State College of Commerce and Economics in Bergen gives an examination in commercial subjects.

Teachers at the elementary and continuation schools are graduates of special teachers' training colleges.

Secondary school teachers are university graduates. There are two teacher classifications: The *"adjunkt"*, who teaches in the "realskole", and the *"lektor"*, who teaches in both the "realskole" and the "gymnas". They study at the University for $3\frac{1}{2}$–4 years and $5\frac{1}{2}$ years respectively, and are required to take three optional subjects either in the humanities or the sciences. One of the subjects may be deplaced by physical culture or by an examination from the teachers' training college. The practical and theoretical training is given by the "Pedagogical Seminary" at a 6-month post-graduate course.

The entire educational system is placed under the Ministry of Church and Education. Special boards of education act as consultants to the Ministry. The teacher organizations, which frequently enjoy a 100 per cent membership, work actively and in harmonious co-operation with the authorities in matter of pedagogic interest.

In recent years a number of *parent-teacher associations* have been formed, and in the secondary schools *student councils* have become general. This might be the beginning of greater activity on the part of two groups that have not been heard much in the school debate, which until now has been largely dominated by the teachers and the politicians.

Students in front of the main buildings of the University of Oslo.

SCIENCE AND RESEARCH

SCIENTIFIC AND HUMANISTIC studies in Norway are associated with a number of institutions subsidized by the State and located throughout the country, the largest and most important being at Oslo, Bergen and Trondheim.

In the capital are the *University of Oslo* (founded 1811) which is Norway's central seat of learning, and the *Norwegian Academy of Science and Letters* (1857), the most prominent learned society in the country. *Bergens Museum* (1825) is engaged in research and museum work primarily appertaining to western Norway. The university activities which it formerly carried on in various fields, have now been transferred to the *University of Bergen* (1946). Bergen is also the seat of the *State College of Commerce and Economics* (1936). At Trondheim is the oldest of Norwegian learned associations, the *Royal Norwegian Society of Sciences* (1760) with a museum and library, and the *State University College of Technology* (1906). *The State University College of Agriculture* (1854, reorganized 1897) is situated at Ås, near Oslo, and important museums are to be found at Stavanger and Tromsø.

The Institute for Comparative Research in Human Culture, (Oslo, 1920, planned and organized by Dr. Fr. Stang) was founded after the first World War to facilitate the re-establishment and promotion of scientific cooperation on international lines. It invites lecturers, Norwegian and foreign, and endeavours to solve specific

problems related to the common foundation of an interrelation between the different civilizations of the world. With funds bequeathed by the late Chr. Michelsen, who was Prime Minister of Norway in 1905, the *Chr. Michelsens Foundation for Science and Intellectual Fredom* (Bergen, 1924) started its activities in 1929 with a view to promoting mutual understanding between social classes, nations, and races, through scientific work and in other ways.

The University of Oslo, which has formed the basis for all later scientific work in Norway, was created at great sacrifice in times which were critical for Norway's national existence, and humanistic research is still largely occupied with national subjects seen from historical points of view — old Norwegian and Northern culture and language (esp. the Saga period), with its survivals, being in the forefront. Representative of the research of three succesive generations in this field are P. A. Munch, Sophus Bugge, and Magnus Olsen, who is the leading research scholar in Norway's linguistic and cultural development during the earliest centuries of her history. Research work is proceeding on broad European lines, and some scientists have particularly stressed the importance of elucidating the interplay between Norse culture and that of the outside world in the Middle Ages, i. e. the culture of the Anglo-Saxons, the Celts, and of continental Europe. Fertile fields for study have been found in national folklore, the runic inscriptions, place names, popular dialects, and the monuments of regional culture, of which there are important collections in the museums at Bygdøy, Oslo and at Maihaugen near Lillehammer. In archeology the richest discoveries have been those from the Arctic stone age culture ("Komsa" culture, Finnmark), and the Viking ships from Gokstad and Oseberg, which are now in the museum at Bygdøy, Oslo.

Humanistic studies of more international scope are chiefly connected with the University of Oslo where, *inter alia*, linguistics (comparative as well as Oriental) and philology, classical and modern, are well represented. Cf. also the two research institutes mentioned above.

It was with pure mathematics *(Nils Henrik Abel)* that Norway, after her re-birth in 1814, made her first important contribution to exact science, since when mathematics, represented by *Sophus Lie* and others, has always occupied a leading position at the University of Oslo. In the field of medicine may be noted the discovery, by *Armauer Hansen*, at Bergen, of the lepra bacillus.

Natural science in Norway has concentrated largely on solving problems connected with the geographical and physical conditions of the country. Its geomorphology, its rocks and loose layers of soil have constantly occupied many of her most prominent scientists, and, in later decades, the field has come to include the Arctic and Antarctic regions (Svalbard, Jan Mayen, East-Greenland, Antarctic islands). The so-called "Oslo-region", in particular, has become famous through the geological work of the late *W. C. Brøgger* and his many pupils and collaborators. The problems of Alpine Norway, which belongs to the Caledonian-Norwegian chain, have called for co-operation between British and Norwegian geologists, both at Oslo and Bergen. The zoological and botanical investigations in Norway during the last 100 years have brought to light highly interesting affinities between her fauna and flora and those of Iceland, Greenland, North America and Sibiria.

The zoological discoveries of *Michael Sars* and the Norwegian North Atlantic Expedition of 1876—78 founded Norwegian marine research which, in conjunction with the great Polar expeditions, has developed considerably, through the work of *Fridtjof Nansen*, *Bjørn Helland-Hansen* and others. Bergen has for years been a centre of oceanographic research. A specific field is the practical-scientific research concerned with salt-water fisheries and their connection with oceanography and plankton production *(Johan Hjort, H. H. Gran* and others). Permanent stations for the study of ocean life are situated at Drøbak on the Oslofjord, in the neighbourhood of Bergen, and at Trondheim.

Most important, not only for Scandinavia but for the whole world, has been the so-called "Bergen-school" of meteorology and weather-forecasting, founded by *Vilhelm Bjerknes* during and after the first World War.

Bjerknes, through his work on dynamic meteorology and hydrography etc. is acknowledged as an international leader in theoretical work in these fields.

The study of past climatic changes during the glacial and postglacial eras was founded by the Norwegian botanist, *Axel Blytt*, in 1876. Through the work of Swedish and Danish scientists, Blytt's ideas were developed along modern lines, and the study of climatic changes in connection with pollen-analysis has to-day assumed great importance for biological, archaeological and geological research throughout the world.

The appointment of the Geophysical Commission of 1918 led to the constitution of a technical Council for Geophysical Problems. Norway is favourably situated for the study of earth-magnetism and the Aurora Borealis. The road to the study of the former was early opened at the University *(Chr. Hansteen)* and much has been built, so far as the latter is concerned, on the foundations laid by *Kr. Birkeland*, especially by *C. Størmer* and *L. Vegard*. Cosmic physics has also progressed, and a special observatory has been built at Tromsø for the study of the Aurora Borealis, earth-magnetism and atmospheric electricity.

The University of Oslo has transferred its departments of mathemathics and natural science from the centre of the city to Blindern, where a group of new buildings with modern laboratories (physics, chemistry, theoretical astrophysics) has been erected. Since 1911, the museums of natural science and a number of laboratories have had their buildings in the Botanical Garden at Tøyen in the eastern part of the capital. The University of Bergen, founded on the institutions of Bergens Museum, has set up new laboratories for geophysics (with a cyclotron), biochemistry and plant-physiology.

In addition to the State and local subsidies, there are funds from foundations formed with voluntary subscriptions and legacies. The chief of these is the Fridtjof Nansen Foundation and its affiliated funds.

Expert advice is available to young students wishing to plan a career.

A well-equipped and up-to-date municipal hospital is the Drammen sykehus.

MEDICAL AND SOCIAL SECURITY

AT SOME TIME or other most persons fall victim to illnesses which render them unfit for work for a longer or shorter period.

The great advances of medical science during the past generation have, on the one hand, made it possible to prevent and to cure many more diseases than formerly. On the other hand, however, both prevention and treatment have become much more complicated, and more costly than before. The largest part of the population does not therefore have the financial reserve to go through an extended period of illness without difficulty.

If the supporter of a family or the housewife is disabled, if unemployment strikes or if a person has to retire as the consequence of age, much the same situation arises.

A society which desires to provide all its members with a certain degree of social and financial security and which wants to protect itself to the greatest possible extent against those interrupions and irregularities caused by illness, disability, old age, accident, unemployment etc. must therefore create such medical and social legislation and institutions that all members of society, regardless of income, sex or age may benefit by them. A system of this kind, when effectively organized, does not mean the laying aside of "idle capital" but the safeguarding of a nation's greatest asset, the men, women and children who constitute its productive capacity.

It is this well known philosophy that provides the basis for the medical and social legislation in Norway. The most important part of the system is *Health Insurance* introduced in 1911 on an obligatory basis now covering between 75 % and 80 % of the population and providing for medical attention, hospital treatment, sickness and maternity cash benefit, funeral grants etc.

The *accident insurance* includes practically all workers and provides for medical attention, hospital treatment and compensation payment to people incapacitated as a result of an accident and to widows and dependents. The *old age pension system* was introduced in 1936 and provides for pensions for all persons on reaching the age of 70, subject to certain income limits. *Child allowances* were introduced in 1947 providing for the payment of kr. 180 (£ 9) per year for all children after the first regardless of the parents' income.

The *uneployment* insurance introduced in 1938 provides for payment of uneployment benefit up to a maximum of 15 weeks per year.

Special legislation covers blind, deaf, disabled, feebleminded, epileptics and individuals suffering from tuberculosis or chronic mental disease.

Great stress is at the present time being put on improving housing conditions and also on the rehabilitation of the partly disabled and on improving the employment machinery with the aim of utilizing to the most effect the manpower available.

*Leif Eiriksson, the discoverer of Amerika, sights land. After the painting
by Chr. Krohg in the National Gallery, Oslo.*

EXPLORATION

N ORWAY's geographical position and conditions of
life fit her people admirably for Polar exploration. Their
early colonization of the Faroe Islands, the Orkneys and
Iceland, and their discovery of Greenland, Svalbard
(Spitzbergen) and North America, which was reached
by *Leif Eiriksson* about 1000 A. D., is an indication of
their ancient tradition as daring seafarers. They were
also responsible for the medieval conception of European
Arctic geography.

In 1827, the Norwegian geologist Dr. Keilhau began
the scientific exploration of Svalbard, and the Norwegian
North Atlantic Expedition of 1876—78 carried out research work over considerable areas and visited, *inter alia*,
Jan Mayen and Svalbard. In 1888, *Fridtjof Nansen* with
five companions crossed the inland ice of Greenland for
the first time, using skis and ski-sledges. From 1893
to 1896, Nansen led the first epoch-making "Fram"
expedition, in the course of which he undertook a sledge
journey, with his companion *Hj. Johansen*, lasting 15
months and reached 86° 14' lat., the northernmost point
attained up to that time. The "Fram", under the command of *Otto Sverdrup*, sailed to 85° 57', farther north
than any ship has been before or since. From 1898 to
1902, Captain Sverdrup led the second "Fram" expedition, this time to the Polar archipelago west of Greenland. New land, with a total area of about 200,000 sq.kms.,
was discovered and mapped, and important scientific

collections were made. The geographical results obtained were greater than those of any expedition since
the time of Franklin.

From 1903 to 1906, *Roald Amundsen* in the "Gjøa"
achieved the distinction of being the first man to navi-
gate the North West Passage. In order to determine the
position of the Magnetic Pole he made continuous magnetic observations over a period of 19 months.

In South Polar regions, Norwegian whalers had, as
early as 1893, penetrated farther south into West Ant-
arctica than anyone before them, and from 1898 to 1900,
Carsten Borchgrevink began the scientific exploration
of the South Polar continent and was the first man to
spend a winter on the Antarctic mainland.

In 1907, Fridtjof Nansen had proposed a new scientific exploration of the North Polar region, based mainly
on the principles of the first "Fram" expedition. Roald
Amundsen took up the idea, but after Peary's discovery
of the North Pole, he changed his plans and made an
expedition to the Antarctic, starting his sledge journey
on the Ross Barrier from the point where Borchgrevink
had landed earlier. On December 15th 1911, Amundsen
with five companions reached the South Pole, where he
planted the Norwegian flag.

Roald Amundsen had to postpone his attempt to reach
the North Pole for many years because of the First
World War. He then built the Polar vessel "Maud"

Fridtjof Nansen,
after a drawing by Erik Werenskiold.

been active in regions other than the Arctic and Antarctic. In the 1870's *C. A. Bock* led British and Dutch financed expeditions to Sumatra as well as the Siamese expedition to Laos. *Carl Lumholtz* (1851—1922) explored Queensland during the period 1880—1884 and later lived for many years with isolated Indian tribes in North West Mexico collecting very valuable ethnological material. In 1947 *Thor Heyerdahl,* the young Norwegian scientist (1914—) set out on a highly adventurous drift across the Pacific. He started with five companions fram Callao in Peru and after 101 days, during which his raft (the "Kon-Tiki") sailed nearly 5,000 miles, landed on the Tuamoto Islands. Heyerdahl undertook the voyage to support his theory that certain areas in the Mid-Pacific were colonised by Indians sailing from the East.

Roald Amundsen,
Norway's great Arctic explorer.

and, in 1920, forced the North East passage. The "Maud" was the third ship to accomplish this feat. She carried on but was delayed by ice and damage and did not enter the ice east of Wrangel Island until 1922. The drift northward proved disappointing; the "Maud", however, returned from her three years in the ice with a rich scientific harvest, collected under the leadership of *dr. H. U. Sverdrup.*

Amundsen met his death in the Arctic in 1928 in an attempt to rescue the Italian Nobile by air.

Norway has continued to play an active part in Antarctic exploration, notably with the four "Norvegia" expeditions which were made between 1927 and 1931. The "Norvegia", under the command of Major *Gunnar Isachsen,* completely circumnavigated the South Polar Continent and the coastal regions were extensively mapped from the air by Captain *Riiser-Larsen* and Captain *Lützow-Holm.* Norwegian explorers have also

The famous "Fram", Nansen's and Amundsen's ship, which is now preserved in its museum at Bygdøy near Oslo.

The "Kon-Tiki" balsa raft under sail in the Pacific Ocean.

Winter is a glorious time!

OUTDOOR LIFE

NORWAY is sparsely populated and her countryside bears so comparatively few marks of human activity that it is not surprising to find her people's attitude to Nature and open air life very different from that of the more densely populated parts of Europe.

Even today, when Norway may be regarded as an advanced and well-developed industrial country, she has few large towns. Her industries, too, are in many cases situated in the country and the towns themselves are set, almost without exception, in unspoiled natural surroundings. They are, so to speak, "enclosed by open space". It is only natural, then, that the life of even the townspeople is influenced considerably by their close contact with Nature. It takes less than an hour to penetrate far into the forest from the largest city in Norway and the great majority of her towns may justifiably be called idyllic garden cities, free from slums or densely built areas. They stand for the most part at the water's edge and access to the open sea is usually no more than a matter of minutes.

These geographical and ethnological factors explain why Norwegians, summer and winter, have an instinctive love for Nature and open air life. It is not always motivated by interest in a particular sport, but simply by an urge to use Nature to the full on sea, in the forests and in the mountains. There are endless opportunities and all are open to Norwegian and foreigner alike.

Generally speaking, this open air life does not call for much impedimenta or costly accessories and very little special equipment is needed. The primary requirements are stout boots, a rucksack and good warm ordinary clothes for the winter, which is severe, as well as a fishing rod and some ski-ing material. All these are well within the reach of every Norwegian, for in this respect Norway's "standard of living" is very far advanced indeed.

Long and strenuous tours in the mountains, on ski or on foot, are undertaken by the young all the year round and not infrequently by their elders as well, provided they are in good training. It is a primitive and a simple life and one can choose either to sleep out with a tent and a sleeping-bag (which can be carried by dog sledge in winter if necessary) or use the tourist huts and crofters cottages. The countryside is open to all without hindrance and long tours through the forests may be undertaken by anyone. In general it is not difficult to find a night's lodgings at the small farms and cottages. There is fishing to be found practically everywhere and

*A dog sledge makes the skier independent of hotel accomodation
in the mountains.*

"A hiker's paradise in every sense of the word."

Paddling among the thousands of islands along the coast combines good sport and an ideal open air life.

even if large catches are not always to be made, it is generally possible, given the necessary equipment, to provide oneself with enough for a meal. In the late summer and during the autumn there is a rich variety of berries to be found on the high plateaus and moors—bilberries, whortleberries and cloudberries, the bear's favourite food. The best weather for mountain or forest tours is generally in early summer or late winter.

Cycle tours are a recreation for the summer. Youth Hostels are to be found at carefully planned intervals throughout the greater part of Southern Norway and camping sites, with watchmen and the usual facilities such as water and cooking hearths, have been established all over the country. These camping places are mostly used by motorists but they are open to all and the charges are very modest.

Holiday life along the coast, particularly the relatively warm south coast, has perhaps a more conventional and international atmosphere than elsewhere in Norway. From June to the end of August there is a bustle and an activity along the coast which has to be seen to be believed. One does not have to seek far for the reason.

The winter is long and most Norwegians seize the opportunity to take their fill of what the winter has denied to them—sunshine and light and warmth. The light nights are an especial source of joy and it is significant that many Norwegians, instead of remaining at home or going to hotels, move farther afield, sailing, rowing or canoeing. Sailing in the summer in Norway is not so much a regatta sport as a recreation and a source of practical value.

Canoeing is growing in popularity from year to year and many canoes now carry sails which enable them to reach the sea itself as well as the narrowest and shallowest waters.

Angling.

Norway offers excellent opportunities for fishing. Innumerable rivers run down to the coast, making it possible for salmon and sea trout to move inland from the sea. In the higher altitudes are lake after lake where trout, grayling and red char thrive. In the lowland

Fly fishing for trout in a mountain lake.

fishing and the number of active fishermen has been growing constantly. This, in turn, has led to a reduction in the stock of fish but both the authorities and private individuals have organized fish-breeding on a scale sufficiently large to make up for the depletion.

Modern means of communication have made it possible for fishermen to reach the most distant parts of the country and ideal spots are no longer easy to find. One may still, however, be certain almost anywhere of filling one's basket with good fish during the seasons and it is still possible, with luck, to find places where fishermen have not penetrated, and where the fisherman's dreams really come true.

Many of the best inland fishing districts belong to the State. Here fishing is open to all Norwegian citizens on payment of 5 kroner for a licence. For foreign nationals the charge is 25 kroner.

Trout vary greatly in size from one part of the country to another and in the more low lying districts, a fish of more than 2 lbs. is rare. Stocks are too large and growth is consequently slow. On the other hand, pike

waters pike, perch, fresh-water herring and other fish are found.

In the last century Norway was a paradise for the few who were interested in fishing at that time. The fish had not seen an artifical fly and every river offered lively sport. The ever-increasing popularity of outdoor life, however, has led to a steady rise in popularity for

Two fine specimens of sea trout caught on dry fly in the Lærdal river.

61

in these districts attain a weight of as much as 30 lbs. In the mountain districts trout weighing from 4 to 8 lbs. are far from rare, even in these days, and red char and grayling attain a size giving excellent sport.

Conditions for salmon and sea-trout fishing are different. All along the coast there are good rivers, some of them renowned for their outstanding fishing. The rights are, as a rule, in private hands and are hired out. Where the rights are owned by hotels the guests are usually permitted to fish without special charges.

Salmon can be found up to 70 lbs. in weight and in many of the rivers of western Norway the sea-trout, too, attain a considerable size.

The fishing season in Norway varies from district to district. In the mountains, at altitudes between 2,500 ft. and 4,000 ft. above sea level, the best time is as a rule from the middle of July to the end of August. From 1,500 ft. above sea level to 2,500 ft. good fishing can be obtained from 1st July to the middle of September. Below 1,500 ft. the season begins as early as the end of May and the best time is to the beginning of July and again from the middle of August to the first week or so in September.

In 1948 the Norwegian Travel Association and the Norwegian Shooting and Fishing Association published "Where to fish in Norway", giving more detailed information about the opportunities for fishing in Norway.

Shooting.

It is somewhat difficult to write about Shooting and the opportunities for this sport in Norway at present, as new legislation is impending and until the Act comes into force, it is not easy to forecast the regulations covering property and Shooting.

Nature has provided Norway with excellent facilities for every form of the chase. There is elk in profusion in the large forest regions from the south to the north and many animals are shot every year. Shooting rights are partly in the hands of the State and partly in private ownership, but as a rule they are not difficult to obtain. The Norwegian Shooting and Fishing Association is always ready to help foreign sportsmen interested in stalking elk, which is a strenuous pursuit, demanding strength and stamina.

The same may be said of reideer stalking, too, which is perhaps the most exciting and fascinating of all. The reindeer always keep above the forest line and invariably move against the wind. One must cover much ground, therefore, before getting within range, but reindeer-hunting in the Norwegian mountains, on the rook of the world so to speak, has a charm which is all its own. Stag is also found west of Bergen and north towards Trondheim. This, too, demands a high degree of physical fitness.

A wild reindeer.

English setter pointing ptarmigan.

Foxes are plentiful in Norway at present and afford good sport. Wolf, lynx and wolverine are to be found in the northern counties but are less numerous than they were. There are still a few bears but they have unfortunately become a rarity.

The most popular game are hare, for which dogs are used, and grouse, which are shot in the autumn, almost invariably with pointers. Nothing can be more exhilarating than the mountain air at this time of year, when everything is clad in warm autumnal colours.

In the forests are found wood-grouse, black-grouse, hazel-grouse and woodcock and many species of duck inhabit the forest lakes and pools. Reindeer used occasionally to be encountered, but they have moved to the far North in recent years. All in all, however, the stocks of larger game in Norway are more stable than the stocks of small game, which fluctuate greatly from year to year, partly because of disease, partly through lack of adequate game administration.

Yachting.

Few countries possess so long and varied a coast as Norway. The distance from Oslo in the south to Kirkenes in the north is 1,452 nautical miles and the actual length of the coastline, taking in the larger islands, is no less than 17,000 miles—more than half the circumference of the earth.

The deep fjords account for a great part of this coastline, which is so well protected by islands and skerries that the coastal waters are, generally speaking, calm and safe.

Because of the great distances involved and the cold climate, Northern Norway is rarely visited by those who sail for pleasure, but yachtsmen who take the trouble to go north are amply rewarded by the magnificent scenery.

Norwegian yachting is concentrated, for the most part, in the waters between Kristiansand S. and the Oslofjord, where the weather is more stable and the air and sea warmer. Here the yachtsman can sail in sheltered waters for practically the entire distance inside islands and skerries and there are many calm sounds and creeks which provide ideal anchorages.

In the summer months, the winds usually blow from the S.S.E. during the forenoon, but gradually swing to the S.W. in the early evening and drop completely towards night. The currents generally run westwards and are strongest between 4 and 6 miles from shore. They seldom, however, exceed 2 to 3 knots in speed.

The Oslo fjord, which is 56 nautical miles in length, is the centre of Norwegian sailing. Its outer part is broad and open, but here, too, islands and skerries provide safe anchorages. Hankø, where the more important regattas are held, stands on this stretch.

At the very end of the fjord is Oslo, where the Royal Norwegian Yacht Club has its clubhouse ("Dronningen"). The R.N.Y.C. has 3,500 members and more than 900 craft on its register. Its Patron is H.M. King Haakon and its Honorary President H.R.H. the Crown Prince Olav. The Crown Prince plays a very active part in the life of the Club, both ashore and afloat.

With so keen an interest in sailing and such admirable natural facilities, it is not surprising that Norwegian yacht building has long held an international reputation. Names such as Colin Archer, Sinding, Johan Anker and Bjarne Aas are known wherever sailing is practised and yachtsmen foregather.

International 6-metres class racing in the Oslo fjord.

Other sports and games.

The Norwegian season for outdoor summer activities lasts for some six months, starting in the latter half of April. There are good, in some cases excellent, opportunities for most sports and games, and it is a national characteristic that the number of participants is very large in comparison with the number of spectators. An exception to this, however, is Association football, which draws huge crowds, particularly during the autumn. Rugby football, baseball and water-polo are not normally played in Norway. As in most countries, active participation in all kinds of sports and games is growing in Norway and the value of exercise and physical training is stressed by the authorities and the medical profession alike.

Athletics, too, especially field events, are very popular and although Norway has produced few really first class runners, cross-country (orientation) running is one of the most popular of spring activities. All track events, incidentally, have to be held out of doors as no suitable indoor halls are available.

In recent years, horse racing (flat and jumping) has attracted much attention. Meetings are held weekly throughout the season, which is from May to October. Bookmaking is not allowed but bets may be placed with the totalizator. The same applies to the trotting meetings which are especially popular in the rural districts.

Rifle shooting is also popular throughout the country. Gymnastics, too, has many followers and lawn tennis is widely played, particularly in eastern and southern Norway.

The 18 hole Golf Course belonging to the Oslo Golf Club is open from early May until late Autumn and Rowing, Riding, Cycling and Swimming all enjoy a brief, but intensive, season. Fencing, Boxing and Wrestling, being primarily indoor activities, are practised for the most part during the winter months.

Mountaineering.

There are four groups of mountains in Norway of special interest to climbers—*Horungtindene* in the western Jotunheimen, the mountains around the *Norangsfjord* in Sunnmøre, the *Romsdal* mountains and the coastal mountains between *Bodø* and *Lofoten*.

Most climbing is done in the Horungtindene group, where the highest and most striking peak is *Store Skagastølstind*, or "Storen", as it is popularly called. It is the central peak of this great mountain group and is extraordinarily impressive from every side, although the best view is, perhaps, that from Midtmaradalen. The peak has been scaled many times since it was first climbed by Wm. C. Slingsby in 1876 and it is by far the most popular and most frequently attempted in Norway. It is natural therefore, that new ways to the top should be found from time to time and there are now no fewer than 9 alternative ascents. The Horungtindene also provide ample opportunities for brae-climbing and a Climber's Guide Book (in English) has been published by Norsk Tindeklub (The Norwegian Mountainering Club) dealing with this mountain group, which can be approached by way of the Sognefjord.

The "Sunnmøre Alps" (the mountains around Norangsfjord) have an overwhelming beauty, with their confusion of peaks and jagged, needle-sharp summits and are unexcelled in Norway for wild and thrilling grandeur. Slingsby discovered this climbers' paradise in 1876, when he ascended the Kolås peak and from that time on, British climbers have been regular visitors to

Cross-country running combines good sport with useful practice in orientation.

(Pictures see next page.)

The 18-hole golf course of the Oslo Golf Club is situated near the beautiful Lake Bogstad.

The famous Store Skagastølstind seen from the ascent to Vesle Skagastølstind.

Not far from Oslo, the "Kolsås Wall" offers splendid training grounds for climbers.

Nordfjord and have made many brilliant ascents. Among the most interesting peaks are *Slogjen, Smørskredtindene, Kviteggen* and *Kolaastind.*

The Romsdal mountains—*Romsdalshorn, Trolltindene* and *Vengetindene*—have a special place among the many Norwegian mountain ranges, for they form the setting to a valley through which, from time immemorial, one of the main arteries of communication that link the county of Møre with Eastern Norway has run. Here, more clearly than anywhere else, the complete transition from almost tropical flora in the valley to the snow and ice of the summits and high crags can be seen. According to a local tradition, there was a small tarn at the summit of Romsdalshorn in which there lay a golden bowl that would become the property of the first man to achieve the ascent. It is not impossible that this prospect tempted the Romsdal dalesmen through the years to attempt the climb. This group can now be reached by water via the Romsdalsfjord to Åndalsnes or by rail from the south.

In the county of Nordland, the main crags are situated along the coast from Bodø to Lofoten. The stupendous mountain mass rises sheer from the sea and has justly been celebrated in song and story for its wild beauty.

*The most spectacular
winter sports event is
"Holmenkollen Day".*

Even those who have seen Hardanger, Sogn, Nordfjord and Sunnmøre cannot fail to be thrilled by these soaring heights. The most interesting peaks, from the mountaineers point of view, are *Stetind, Åslitind, Strandåtind, Husbyviktind,* and *Svolvaergeita.* They can be reached by boat from many places along the coast. Many cragsmen equip themselves with tents or hire a small fishing boat for accommodation and transport when in this region because of the long distances between the hotels.

Climbing in Norway generally means climbing on dry rock rather than braes. Those primarily interested in brae-climbing will, however, find excellent opportunities on the Horungtindene and Jostedalsbreen, the largest glacier on the European mainland.

Norway is more fortunate, from the point of mountaineering, than Central Europe in that natural hazards arising out of avalanches or falling boulders are very infrequent. The reason lies in the comparatively even temperature which prevails throughout the day in Norway during the climbing season. In Nordland, the best time is between Midsummer and the middle of August. The southern mountain groups are best attempted between the beginning of July and mid-August.

The length of the day's march may be regulated so that one can start out in the morning and be back again by the evening. Equipment consists of ordinary practical sports wear, greased-leather boots (iron-shod or rubber-soled), as well as the necessary climbing gear.

Winter sports.

Ski-ing has its roots deep in the Norwegian people. It is mentioned in the mediaeval sagas as a royal sport and rock carvings, as well as the finds of skis buried deep in the bogs, prove that ski-ing has been practised in Norway from times immemorial. In the past, it was primarily a means of locomotion, but nowadays its first use is for sport or recreation.

It was the peasants from Telemark who introduced competitions in slalom and jumping in the middle of the 19th century and thereby gave ski-ing its present widespread popularity. It at once became the predominant sport of the people and the first real Christmas present that Norwegian children receive is a pair of skis, which may explain why they are so often said to be born with skis on their feet!

In late winter, the mountains are covered with the tracks left by climbing and descending skiers.

Twisting through one of the gates in a slalom race.

Fridtjof Nansen's epic journey across Greenland on ski in 1888 brought ski-ing to the notice of other countries and it has spread from Norway to every land where snow is to be found. Norway may therefore justifiably be called "the home of ski-ing". Few countries have so many facilities to offer, not only to the experienced skier but to the beginner as well. In some parts of the country, the snow falls as early as October and remains until April or May. In the mountains of southern Norway, one can be certain of ski-ing from November to April or even later.

In the north ski-ing cannot start before February because of the winter darkness, but there is compensation in the fact that conditions remain wellnigh perfect until nearly the end of May.

The Norwegian terrain can cater for every type of skier. There are gentle slopes for the beginner and long steep runs for the more advanced. For those who are interested in jumping, there are hills of all sizes up to the very largest, where one can swoop through the air for 240 to 270 feet or more. The world-famous Holmenkollen Competition, which is held in beautiful surroundings just outside Oslo, attracts up to 100,000 spectators. It is the ambition of every skier to take part in this competition, which was first held in 1892 and is always attended by the Royal Family.

In the first four Olympic Winter Games, Norway has led the world in the Ski-ing Events. It is her national sport and every Norwegian—young or old, rich or poor—plays an active part.

The other great winter sport, skating, has also been practised in Norway from times immemorial and Norwegian skaters have played a predominant role in both the World Championships and the Olympic Games. Many large scale competitions, long distance and figure skating, are held annually throughout the country and attract enormous crowds.

Ice Hockey and Bandy (a Scandinavian form of ice hockey with 11 men a side) are steadily increasing in popularity. Local authorities have ensured that these sports can be

A perfect jump.

Every type of ski terrain can be found in Norway — here is a competitor in a downhill race.

The great highland plateaus are ideal for long trips on skis.

Mountains, snow and sunshine combine to give the skiers health and colour.

Ski sailing is a thrilling adventure.

pursued after working hours in the dark winter months by providing the pitches with adequate flood-lighting. Many jumping hills, too, are artificially illuminated and in the Oslo district and other places where there is much ski-ing activity, care has been taken to mark the tracks so clearly that people can find their way without difficulty.

For winter tourists there are many first class hotels in those regions where an abundance of snow and comparatively settled weather conditions offer perfect ski-ing. The pleasures of good food, good society, music and dancing are always greater after a long day in the open air under the stimulating rays of a sun reflected from myriads of glittering snow crystals, but for those who prefer a holiday in complete privacy and in closer contact with Nature, facilities also exist for living in the genuine Norwegian style, i. e. in a log cabin, preparing ones own meals and doing exactly as one pleases, free from all social ties. Special agencies will put you in touch with owners of private log cabins willing to let their often very comfortable and well-equipped places for the period required. To people with the real open-air instinct, nothing can surpass the feeling of complete freedom and independence in surroundings of unforgettable beauty and peace.

Carrying Norway's colours in an international long distance race.

ECONOMIC LIFE
Agriculture.

OF THE TOTAL AREA (324,000 sq. kms.) of the country, 7,600,000 hectares is timberland, 824,000 hectares is cultivated farm land, 237,000 hectares natural pasture and grazing grounds, and 90,000 hectares cultivated pasture land. 800,000 hectares of the undeveloped area is arable land.

The Norwegian farms are, generally speaking, very small. All told, there are 214,000 independently owned farms having each a cultivated area of more than 0.5 ha. The average size of these small-holdings is 4.3 hectares. There are only 25,000 farms having a cultivated area of more than 10 hectares. Most farms have, besides, some timber land and natural grazing grounds. In some parts of the country there are large natural mountain pastures which are used primarily for sheep, goats and reindeer.

In Norway the farms are owned by the peasants themselves. Very few farms are operated on a tenant basis. Many of the small farmers have to eke out their livelihood by taking other work. In the Eastern Provinces and in the Province of Trøndelag the most common combination is farming and timberlogging. In the coastal districts of Western Norway farming is usually combined with fishing.

The climate and the nature of the soil vary greatly, and as a consequence the conditions for farming differ widely. In the most fertile agricultural areas — the broad valleys of the Eastern Provinces, the flat lowlands of Jæren in South-Western Norway, and the regions around the Trondheim Fjord — all-round farming is carried on under favourable conditions. In these areas is grown most of the domestically produced grain. In ordinary years, barley is cultivated with satisfactory results up to 1,700—2,000 feet above sea level in the Southern Provinces, and as far north as Alta at 70° North. This is the northern-most point in the world at which grain is grown. Potatoes are grown everywhere with excellent crop yields. The climatic conditions are particularly well suited to the growing of grass and other green fodder. Therefore, the cultivation of animal fodder holds a prominent position in plant production in Norway.

In spite of the far northerly geographical position and the short summers, the crop yields in Norway are

considerable. Here are some figures showing average yields in tons per ha.: Spring Wheat 2.31 — Rye 2.20 — Barley 2.43 — Oats 2.40 — Potatoes 22.42 — Turnips 40.23 — Fodder Roots 48.87 — Hay 5.32.

As already mentioned, the cultivation of grass and animal fodder holds a prominent position in the plant production. In consequence, animal husbandry is an important part of Norwegian farming.

There are two breeds of Norwegian horses — one medium size (*Dølehest*, the breed typical of the eastern valleys) and one smaller (*Fjordhest*, of the coastal breed). The cattle are usually of domestic Norwegian breed. All breeds of Norwegian cattle are good milk cows for their size. Norwegian breeds of sheep include the *Dala* sheep and the *Rygja* sheep. The Cheviot breed, which was originally introduced from England, is also used. Practically all the goats are of local, domestic breeds.

The health of the livestock in Norway is usually excellent. Foot-and-mouth disease does not exist, and tuberculosis among the livestock is very rare.

Dairy farming is satisfactorily developed. There are, all told, 618 co-operative dairies, cheese factories and condensed milk factories. Since 1928 the State Grain Monopoly has been in charge of all grain imports. The State has also subsidized the domestic production of grain in various ways.

Both the State and the various agricultural organizations are working actively for the further development of farming in Norway.

The comparatively advanced agricultural education, the research and technical training are all conducted and paid for by the State. Elementary agricultural education is given chiefly by the various provinces, which receive financial support from the State for the purpose.

Both in farming and forestry, modern machinery and implements are being utilized increasingly. The general utilization of such equipment is organized locally through co-operative machine stations. These enterprises are supported by Government loans and subsidies. The State also grants loans and subsidies for the establishment of new small-holdings, the breaking and cultivating of new land, and for ditching and drainage work.

Forestry.

The productive *forest* area of Norway covers some 7.6 million hectares, or nearly one fourth of the total land area. With a population of some 3 million, this is equivalent to a forest area of approximately 2.5 hectares per inhabitant.

The greatest timber areas are found in the South-Eastern Provinces and in the Province of Trøndelag (on

Judging young horses at a Show.

The total annual growth to-day is approximately 12 million solid m³, which is made up of approx. 56 per cent spruce, 24 per cent pine and 20 per cent foliferous species. Most of the foliferous forest timber is birch (Betula odorata and verrucosa). Birch grows also in Northern Norway an here frequently forms belts of shelter forest above the timberline for coniferous species. Otherwise it grows all over the country, partly mixed into the coniferous forests, partly in pure stands of birch forest. The same is the case with aspen (Populus). Other species of foliferous trees that prefer a milder climate — such as oak (Quercus), ash (Fraxinus excelsior), maple (Acer platanoides), linden (Tilia cordata), alderwood (Almus incana and glutinosa), beechwood (Fagus silvatica), an many others — are usually only found in the southernmost parts of the country.

Partly because of the abnormal conditions during and after the war, the exploitation of the forests has varied considerably in recent years, but on the average the felling has been kept within the bounds of the annual growth. Approximately 6 million m³ is sold as timber to sawmills, woodpulp mills, cellulose factories etc., appr. 3 million m³ is used for household purposes, firewood etc.

The most important export products are woodpulp, cellulose and paper, and small quantities of pit props, poles etc. Approximately 80 pct. of the forests in Norway are privately owned about 64 per cent belonging to farmers and 16 per cent

Platinum foxes have provided a good source of income to many farmers.

both shores of the Trondheim Fjord). The productive forest in the inland regions of the South-Eastern Provinces climbs up to 800 metres above sea level, where it meets the sub-mountainous shelter forest. In the Province of Trøndelag the forests grow up to approximately 600 metres above sea level, but the maximum altitude becomes gradually lower farther north and nearer the coastal districts.

Western and Northern Norway are poor forest areas, but there are great possibilities for forest cultivation in the extensive waste-lands of these regions, where forest planting has already been started in a number of places.

As is the case elsewhere in Scandinavia, the forests in Norway are chiefly coniferous, such as spruce (Picea excelsa) and pine (Pinus silvestris). These species form the basis for the pulp and paper industries and the export trade.

From the latest nation-wide survey on the state of Norway's forests, it appears that the net increase in timber volume has been 15—20 per cent during the past 20 years.

to industrial concerns. The remaining 20 per cent belong to the State, to local municipalities, and to parishes. There are in all approx. 121,000 forest properties; 30 per cent of the forest area belong to properties having up to 100 hectares, and 35 per cent to properties having more than 1,000 hectares of forest land.

The public administration of the forests is vested in the Forest Directorate of the Ministry of Agriculture.

The logging operations are carried out during the winter months, and most of the timber is drawn by horse to the river banks and stacked. In the spring the timber is measured and marked, and title is transferred to the purchaser. Then the logs are floated down the rivers to the industrial plants. In recent years trucks and tractors have come into more general use, and new forest roads — for the most part built with Government subsidies — are opening new areas for mechanized transportation of timber.

Advanced education in forestry is given at the Agricultural College of Norway. More elementary forestry education is given at the State Forestry Schools, and to some extent at the agricultural schools.

Timber feller at work.

*Freeing jammed logs in the river
is a tricky job.*

Manufacturing Industries.

Besides agriculture, industry is the most important means of livelihood in Norway, providing a living for approximately 30 per cent of the population.

Although the industrial growth and expansion did not gain impetus until the middle of the 19th century, some branches of industry can be traced back several hundred years. Thus, the lumber industry and the smelting of iron, which are the oldest industries, reached considerable proportions as early as 1500—1600. Quarrying, brickmaking and the production of glass also played an important part at a time when industry was relatively undeveloped. From the eighteen forties onward the textile industry and the engineering industries developed and grew.

In the beginning, industry was based chiefly on the supplying of domestic requirements. The typical export industries, with the exception of the lumber industry, developed at a later date. The basic materials for our most important export industries are found in the forests, in the ore deposits, in the minerals, in the wealth of fish along the extensive coastline, and in the resources of waterpower.

The modern pulp and paper industry dates back to the eighteen seventies, and at about the same time the canning factories began to spring up in the cities along the coast. The electro-chemical industry dates from the turn of the century, when the first carbide furnaces were installed. The carbide industry also formed the basis of a number of other industries, having among other things contributed greatly to the formation and rapid growth of the ferro-alloy industry, which is so important to-day.

The increase in that part of the population which derives its living from industry gives a clear picture of the growing importance of industry in the economic life of the nation. In 1801 barely 6 per cent of the population was engaged in industry, while more than 80 per cent made its living from agriculture. In 1865 the corresponding figures were 15 per cent and 64 per cent respectively, and to-day industry and farming each account for approximately 30 per cent. In order to get a correct picture, one must also take into consideration the fact that the population has been more than tripled in the same period.

As more and more capital was invested per worker, and as ever greater supplies of hydro-electric power became available, the industrial output per worker increased considerably. In 1948, the output of hydro-electric power reached a t otal of nearly 12,300 million KWH, of which industry utilized about 50 per cent.

A relic of bygone days — an old flour mill still in use.

*A cable car carries the workers of the industrial town of Rjukan
to the adjacent mountain plateau.*

The German occupation of Norway during World War II put a temporary stop to further expansion. Large sections of industry were cut off from their sources of supply and their markets. Supplies for the factories were inadequate, and the quality of raw materials and stores deteriorated. There was little or no opportunity for replacement of machinery and equipment, and as time went on, the uneven supply of raw materials and the transportation difficulties also caused considerable loss of operating time. Furthermore, the working tempo was reduced as a result of the poor food situation.

Since the war, the industrial output has increased considerably. Already in 1946 the industrial production index had reached the 1938 level (1938 = 100 points). In 1947 the index showed 125 points. It is chiefly that part of industry which supplies the home market that has brought the index up. The export industry has not yet reached the pre-war level, having been more severely crippled by war damage. The effects of this damage have not yet been completely surmounted.

The iron and metal industry is the branch of industry which employs the greatest number of workers. This industry works essentially for the domestic market, as do the textile and clothing industries.

Of Norwegian export industries may be mentioned first the pulp and paper industry, which exports its products to all parts of the world. In 1948, the export of pulp and paper products accounted for 29 per cent of the total export value of the country. The output was approximately 800,000 tons mechanical woodpulp (dry content 45/100), 350,000 tons cellulose (dry content 90/100), and 450,000 tons cardboard and paper.

In addition to the usual pulp and paper products, a number of new products have been developed, such as staple fibre, rayon etc. Constant and effective research is also bringing out new products.

Mining in Norway is very old, and already in the Middle Ages and during the following centuries considerable ore was mined. In contrast to earlier days when the ore was refined domestically, to-day it is mainly exported. The reason for this is the lack of coal, great quantities of which are required for the reduction of the ore. However, new electric smelting methods have now been developed, and since Norway has an ample supply of labour, the State has started the construction of a large iron and steel plant in Northern Norway.

Some of the export articles in this field are: iron ore, pyrites, cintered iron ore, zinc ore, molybdenum ore and sulphur.

The electro-metallurgical industry is almost exclusively based on export. Cheap hydro-electric power which is obtained from the rivers and waterfalls of the country,

The factories of the Borregaard Company (pulp and paper) flank the Sarpsfossen waterfall.

The Haugland Smelting Works are supplied with power from the hydro-electric power plant at Glomfjord in Nordland.

forms the basis of this industry. In 1939, 147,000 tons ferro-alloys were produced, but to-day the output is considerably less, for the reasons stated above.

Other metals produced are aluminium, copper, nickel and zinc. Production has now practically reached the pre-war level, i. e. 30,000 tons aluminium, 11,000 tons copper, 42,000 tons zinc and 9,000 tons nickel. As a result of plant expansions, the production of aluminium and nickel is expected to increase considerably.

The electro-chemical industry too is based on extensive use of cheap hydro-electric power. The development of this industry is closely identified with the names of two Norwegian inventors, *Birkeland* and *Eyde*. Production is now practically back to the pre-war level, which in 1939 showed the following figures for some of the more important export products: various fertil-

izers (nitrates) 426,500 tons, carbide 70,900 tons, and cyanimide 32,900 tons.

Other typical export industries are the canning and the oil and fat industry. In 1948, Norway exported a total of 33 855 tons canned fish products having a total value of 100 million kroner. (£ 5 mill.) The export of oils and fats (mainly whale oil) for the same year amounted to 301 million kroner. As already mentioned, the export in 1948 of pulp and paper products accounted for 29 per cent of the total exports. Then came oils and fats with 14.5 per cent, metallurgical products with 13.5 per cent, canned fish products with 5.8 per cent, and fertilizers with 4.6 per cent.

Great Britain is the most important single purchaser of Norway's export products, followed by Sweden, the United States and France.

Norway's many waterfalls provide an inexhaustible source of power.

Water power.

Norway is relatively speaking more favourably situated in regard to water power than any other country in the world. Although Norway's resources of power are not, absolutely, the greatest to be found in any one country, yet they rank first in proportion to the population and are the cheapest to develop.

The present population of Norway is well over three million. The aggregate amount of water power, according to official statistics, is computed to be approximately 14 million horse-power on turbine shaft. It must, however, be borne in mind that this estimate is based on a constant supply of power every second throughout the year. So rigorous a standard when applied to the water power of a country, will obviously reduce the number of horse-power far below the quantity actually used, seeing that no industrial or other power consumer has so constant a demand for power. Only two manufacturing industries, viz., nitrogen and aluminium, have a consumption factor approaching 100 per cent.

Electrical energy derived from water-power plants is now employed in practically every industry, in addition to large quantities used for ordinary electrical purposes, private as well as public. Of the water power developed at present 2.8 million kW (about 48 pct.) is employed in the latter manner. As regards its industrial use, the electro-chemical and electro-metallurgical industries in particular consume large quantities of power —at present about 38 pct. of the power, or rather less than the amount used for ordinary electrical purposes. The factories engaged in manufacturing nitrogen products,

6

A big hydro-electric power plant at Nore in Numedal.

carbide, and aluminium, are the largest consumers in this branch of industry. Paper and pulp manufacture consumes at present about 11 pct. of the generated power, and other industries (textiles, foodstuffs and mines) together require about 3 pct. Electricity for the operation of railways, up to the present forming but a small part of the total energy, is included in the above quota of power consumption for public electrical pur-

poses. Progress in this line is at present gathering speed.

The natural facilities for generation of electric energy are so favourable in Norway that the price of power generally is very low. The demand has constantly increased, the average usage being roughly 0,55 HP per capita (in Southern Norway). This comprises only domestic and municipal consumption, including small manufacturing industries as well.

Norwegian water power in general possesses several favourable features which have not only stimulated its utilization for general electrical purposes, but have also made it attractive to interests seeking opportunities for the creation of modern large-scale industries. Such features are that a great number of the falls can be developed at a cheap rate, in fact so cheaply that other countries, whether generating power by water or by fuel, will have difficulty in competing. Another feature is that considerable amounts of power are concentrated in very great single power resources, the greatest one being of about 180,000 effective kW supplied constantly all the year round. Another advantage is that water falls very often are close to the fjords, where suitable sites for factories etc. are available. This feature is of paramount importance because the fjords of Norway are free from ice and deep enough to be navigated by large ocean-going vessels. Thus, the transportation problem, which means so much in rational manufacture, can be solved in an ideal manner.

By developing the water-power resources of Norway, the mechanical, electrical, chemical and construction engineers of the country have produced results which place Norway among the foremost technical nations of the world in their particular sphere.

Shipping.

For centuries Norwegians have looked to the sea for their livelihood and as a means of communication. This is only natural, for 3 out of every 4 Norwegians live within 20 miles of the coast and only 3 pct. of the country is under cultivation. Compared with other nations, a very large percentage of Norway's population is engaged in Shipping, Fishing and Whaling. Of these, Shipping has long provided the greatest revenue. Ever since Norway's first great maritime era, which started in the 9th century with the Viking Age and lasted for three to four hundred years, shipping has played its part in the economic welfare of the nation and exerted a strong influence on her culture.

Although Norwegian shipping has age-old traditions, it was not until the middle of the 19th century that Norwegians virtually became the "sea transporters of the world". Norway then built up the world's third largest merchant fleet, based on her sailing ships, and established many and valuable connections with importers and exporters all over the globe. It was this that laid the foundation for the astonishing expansion which followed.

The latter part of the 19th century saw the establishment by Norwegian shipowners of a number of special trades which were to attain great importance in international maritime trade and Norwegian ships participated from the outset in the tanker as well as in the fruit trade, and opened up markets the world over.

The transition from sail to steam involved sacrifices which strained the economic resources of what was, in effect, a small and relatively poor country, with the result that towards the end of the 19th century Norway saw her merchant fleet lagging behind somewhat in the international development of shipping. However, from the turn of the century until the outbreak of the first World War Norwegian shipping again had a period of expansion, and by 1914 Norway held fourth place among the shipping nations of the world.

The first World War did away with the rest of Norway's sailing ships and concluded the transition to steam. The relatively favourable freight revenue during this period made it possible for the owners to adopt the expensive diesel motors. World War I nevertheless dealt a heavy blow to Norway's merchant fleet. More than 2,000 Norwegian seamen lost their lives and about 1.3 mill. g.r.t., about 50 pct. of the country's tonnage, were lost.

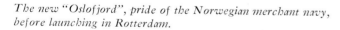

The new "Oslofjord", pride of the Norwegian merchant navy, before launching in Rotterdam.

Launching of the "Thermopylae" (10,000 t.d.w.) biggest ship ever built in Norway.

chant fleet and 18,5 per cent of the total tanker fleet of the world. At the same time more than 1 mill. g.r.t. of the Norwegian merchant fleet were engaged in overseas liner trade. At the outbreak of the second World War the fleet of Norwegian *motorships* had passed 3 mill. g.r.t. and constituted over 62 per cent of the total merchant fleet—compared with 24 per cent as regards world tonnage.

In the two decades between the first and second World Wars, the Norwegian merchant fleet was brought up to nearly 4,9 mill. g.r.t. and by 1939 Norway had regained her pre—1914 position as fourth among the shipping nations of the world.

The influence of Norway's merchant fleet on the national economy may best be illustrated, perhaps, by the fact that, between the two wars, the fleet contributed an average of 30 per cent to the payment of imports, and its revenue was 10 per cent of the national income. It may be pertinent in this connection to mention that in modern times Norway has had a larger foreign trade per capita than any other country with the exception of New Zealand.

When Norway was invaded on April 9th 1940, 80 per cent of the fleet or more than 4 mill. g.r.t —of which 2 mill. g.r.t were in tankers—were outside German controlled waters. Not a single ship failed to seek an Allied port. The fleet immediately joined the Allied war effort.

At the very start of the war in Norway, the Norwegian Government in London, in co-operation with Norwegian owners, established an organisation for the operation of the merchant fleet: "The Norwegian Shipping and Trade Mission"—popularly known as "Notraship"—with its head office in London.

During the war Norwegian seamen and Norwegian shipping maintained and strengthened their reputation from the first World War. Norwegian vessels participated in nearly all amphibian operations in the Western hemisphere as well as in the Pacific. During the invasion of Normandy in 1944, between 50 and 60 Norwegian vessels were engaged in carrying war material across the British Channel. The contribution of the tanker fleet was undoubtedly the most important. During the war, the Norwegian tanker fleet carried about 75 mill. tons of oil products for the Allied forces, and in the most critical period during the Battle of Britain more than 40 per cent of Britain's oil supply was carried in Norwegian tankers.

But war losses were heavy. Of the approximately 30,000 Norwegian seamen in the Allied service some 3,000 lost their lives, and about 2.4 mill. g.r.t.—half the

The breakdown of the freight market in 1920 brought in its train a change in international shipping policy from free competition to protectionism, a tendency particularly alarming to Norwegian interests. Norwegian shipping was faced with the necessity for seeking new fields for its activities if it was to avoid stagnation and ultimate collapse. The solution to this complicated problem was found in a reversal of the former policy by basing the industry on high class tonnage and by resorting to specialization and concentration on particular markets and types of vessels. The steam vessels were, in ever increasing number, being replaced by well equipped and fast, costly motor ships. This tendency to specialization resulted in a sharp increase in the tanker, liner and fruit ship tonnage. The *tanker fleet* flying the Norwegian flag had reached 2 mill. g.r.t. before World War II, i. e. 44 per cent of the total Norwegian mer-

A modern cargo liner.

Captain's day room on a modern cargo liner.

Norwegian merchant fleet at the beginning of the war —was sunk as a result of enemy action.

In view of the significance of the merchant fleet in the national economy it was natural that the rebuilding of the fleet should enjoy high priority in the country's reconstruction programme. The vital importance to Norway of maintaining the great assets represented by her able and well trained seamen and her regular, well-established lines with markets all over the globe, is appreciated by every section of her people.

During the reconstruction of their fleet Norwegian owners have been confronted with a number of problems: the lack of foreign currency has prevented the placing of contracts which would otherwise have been in every way desirable, while the country's own shipyards have had great difficulty in finding skilled labour and materials—particularly steel.

In spite of much delay the Norwegian merchant fleet had reached about 4.5 mill. g.r.t. by the beginning of 1949. Taking into account the tonnage afloat and contracts placed before the outbreak of the last war—approximately 5.5 mill. g.r.t.—it is evident that the prewar level of the fleet will not be reached for some to come.

By January 1949 *tonnage contracted for* by Norwegian owners amounted to 2.2 mill. g.r.t.—12 per cent of which is to be built at Norwegian yards. As much as 39 per cent of the contracts have been placed in Sweden and 38 per cent in the United Kingdom, the balance of the contracts being distributed between Denmark, Belgium, the Netherlands, Italy and Japan. Even though the percentage of contracts placed at Norwegian yards is relatively small, these yards will be working at full capacity for several years to come. Of the new building contracts, about 70 per cent are tankers and the rest dry cargo ships.

Even so, one finds that the programme of new building mentioned will hardly suffice to bring the fleet up to and maintain its prewar standard. Norwegian owners are primarily intent upon the *qualitative* reconstruction of the fleet, for they are well aware that Norway's competitive power in the international freight market is due, first and foremost, to the fleet's quality.

The shipowners have resumed the policy embarked upon between the world wars—qualitative services and specialized ships and trades. In January 1949 about 40 per cent of the fleet were tankers, the rest dry cargo ships, i. e. about the same distribution as before the war. In the course of the next few years, however, the tanker fleet will show a relatively much higher increase than the rest of the fleet, and in 3—4 years the relative percentage of tankers and dry cargo ships will probably be the opposite of what it is today.

Norway occupies a unique position among shipping nations in that 80 per cent of her tonnage is exclusively engaged in trade between foreign ports. Norwegian owners must, therefore, be able to continue to offer first class and cheap service.

The Ports.

Because of the Gulf-Stream Norway's fjords are open the year round. The numerous and well sheltered harbours are sufficiently deep for even the largest vessels and offer excellent anchorages. The approaches are easily navigated and tides and currents are hardly noticeable.

Space does not allow mention of more than 3 of the larger centres of population (Oslo, Bergen, Trondheim) at which modern and well-equipped harbours have been developed.

Oslo Harbour is ideally situated at the head of the Oslo fjord. It is well protected and has more than 20 miles of quays with some 100 cranes of upwards of 100

H. M. the King's motor yacht "Norge".

tons capacity. Because of war damage and the ravages of five years of occupation, the harbour has not yet re-gained its full pre-war efficiency and traffic is still a little under normal. Statistics show that approximately 24,000 calls are made a year, representing about 2,4 mill-ion n.r.t. The considerable importance of Oslo as a port is due, partly to the fact that the city is the centre of the southern Norwegian railway system and partly to her position as the largest shipping centre in the country — a position which she has held for the past quarter of a century.

Bergen handles a considerable transit trade by sea and rail from all parts of the country and her harbour is notable for the very large number of tugboats and local steamers which serve it. Bergen, incidentally, berthed the largest vessel to visit Norway – the U. S. aircraft carrier "Valley Forge". The harbour, which can compete with that of any northern port, has excellent berths and 8½ miles of quays equipped with every modern techni-cal aid. In 1947 there were 45,000 calls with a total tonn-age of more than 4 million n.r.t. As commerce and shipp-ing are the dominating factors in Bergen's economic life, her harbour has a very important role to play.

Trondheim, which stands on the Trondheimsfjord, is the most important trading and commercial centre for the northern part of the country. Her large harbour has built up an extensive transit trade and berthing 's good. The discharging facilities, however, have still some way to go before they reach the same level. Many im-provements have, however, been made since the war and as the large scale projects for expansion gather mo-mentum, the port of Trondheim will undoubtedly be able to satisfy the needs of her transit trade, which is steadily increasing because of the city's excellent rail connection with northern Sweden.

The Fisheries.

Through archeological finds we can catch a glimpse of the methods of fishing employed in Norway in ancient times. Fish-hooks and other tools of stone and bone show that the art of fishing, as it is practised to-day, still has the same fundamental structure that it had ten thousand years ago. Climate, the temperature of the sea, and other factors which influence the movement of the fish have certainly changed from time to time, but not to such an extent that the coastal population of Norway has ever failed to make its living from the sea. Norway has devel-oped some of the most important fisheries in the world. With a total population of 3 million, 80,000 of whom

A glimpse of Oslo harbour.

The fishing fleet leaving a Lofoten harbour.

are employed in the fishing industry, Norway supplies each year an average of 2,500 million lbs. of fish to the world's foods stocks. This average puts Norway on a level with U.S.A. and Great Britain, who also provide approximately the same amount. Only Japan and, probably, the Soviet Union, catch more.

The Norwegian fishing industry is first and foremost based on two varieties of fish — the cod and the herring — which each year return to Norway's coast in order to spawn. In good years, the number of fish at the time of spawning reach practically incalculable proportions.

Most widely-known outside Norway itself it the yearly season of cod fishing, when shoals of cod are concentrating in the waters outside the Lofoten islands. The Norwegian-Arctic stock of cod has its home in the ocean to the north and east of Norway, the so-called Barents Sea. The fish lives on these arctic banks until it becomes mature at the age of 6—12 years, when it swims westward and southward to the Norwegian coast. There it finds the temperature and current conditions suitable for spawning, and there the milliards of larvae will hatch. To show the enormous quantities of cod appearing in Lofoten, can be mentioned a single shoal which was observed in 1947, and which was measured to be 7 miles long and 3—4 miles broad. This one shoal probably contained at least 100 million fish.

The Lofoten fisheries are said to be the greatest cod fisheries in the world. In the course of the 12 weeks season, the Norwegian fishermen catch between 130 and 300 million lbs. of cod, with a yearly average of 170 mill. lbs. Through many centuries this colossal catch has formed the basis of one of Norway's most important export products. The Norwegian stockfish and later the split cod have become valued food in Europe, with the biggest export going to the Latin countries around the Mediterranean. Latin emigrants have brought the taste for these products across the oceans to both continents of America.

As the Norwegian cod is to be found close to land, the Norwegian fishermen are able to use small boats of practically every conceivable design, from motor cutters down to rowing boats. The fishing implements are hand-line, long-lines and net. With about 5,000 vessels, manned by 20—30,000 men, bobbing up and down the sea, a sunny day on the Lofoten fishing-grounds is a most picturesque scene. With a background of snow-capped alpine mountains rising straight from the sea in an unbroken chain for 125 miles, fishing vessels lie side by side as far as the eye can see, and on quiet days the exhaust from thousands of motors sometimes becomes so compact that it forms a curtain between the sun and the sea.

The second of the main fisheries of Norway is the yearly winter season of herring fishing, which commences just around Christmas, and lasts well into the spring. This season is also caused by the fish coming in to spawn The size and importance of the herring fisheries have varied immensely from time to time. We are now in

88

a richer period than ever before. Millions of herrings, in shoals which make the water boil, covering whole areas which measure hundreds of yards across, are caught by the fishermen. In the record year 1948, Norwegian fishermen caught 1,400 million lbs. of this ocean wealth. This means that, if we calculated the catch in meals, Norway could give every living person on the earth a hearty dinner, with enough left over for a snack at breakfast time!

The Norwegian fisheries are, however, not based entirely on these two main seasons. Brisling, fat herring, and mackerel are caught in summer, haddock, halibut and plaice in practically every season. The Norwegian part of the Continental Shelf is a rich feeding-ground for many stationary fish varieties, of which the local stock of cod, which never leaves the coast, is the most important.

The Norwegian fisherman has until recently caught his cod by old-fashioned methods. Having the fish practically on the doorstep, the Norwegians had not seen the need for ocean-going vessels to catch the fish. Therefore, other countries have far exceeded Norway in constructing vessels for cod-fishing in distant waters. Norway's economic situation now demands a satisfactory delivery of fresh fish for export all the year round. One of the main issues in Norwegian fishing politics at present is the question of building a modern and effective trawler-fleet. In recent years the Norwegian canning industry has had a rapid development, and another section of the fishing industry has concentrated on deep-freezing fish for export, which can then be delivered, completely fresh, after months of storage.

A small part of the enormous quantities of herring is exported in its fresh condition, while some is salted. Most of the herring catch, however, is used to produce oil, thus forming the basis of the important margarine industry.

In 1948, Norway exported fish or fish products for 520 million kroner (26 mill. £) while the total export income was 2,000 million kroner (100 mill. £).

Whaling.

The modern industrial adventure called whaling is due to the initiative of Norwegian catchers. They have developed new techniques and found new whaling grounds. They have also been pioneers in evolving methods of utilising the whale.

The first significant step in this development was made when *Sven Foyn* constructed the grenade harpoon, placing a harpoon gun in the bow of a steamboat. Whaling was carried on in Arctic waters and off the Norwegian coast until the end of the last century. Then the stock of whales in these waters became so greatly reduced that whaling no longer paid, and the Norwegian catchers sought new grounds on the other side of the globe and discovered that Antarctic waters offered far richer possibilities. The whaling expeditions were con-

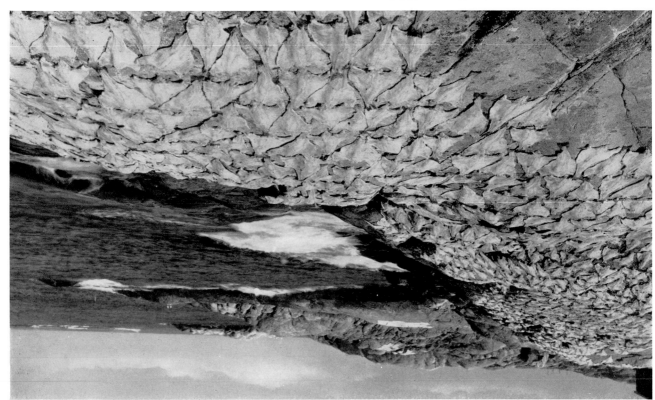

Cod drying in the sun on the cliffs near Kristiansund.

Whale hauled on deck of the floating factory, ready to be cut up for the boilers below deck.

than 30,000 tons of whale oil worth about 3 million pounds sterling in the course of a season of about 4 months.

During the years before the second World War very many countries took part in the whale hunt, which was carried on to such an extent that the stock of whales was reduced to a dangerously low level. In order to prevent the whale from becoming extinct, Norway took the initiative to limit the kill of whales, at the same time passing a law requiring the total utilisation of the whale carcase. In 1937 these endeavours resulted in an international whaling agreement, which remained in force until the outbreak of the second World War.

During the war the Norwegian floating factories rendered the Allies great service as oil tankers, but they suffered heavy losses. At the end of the war, only 3 out of 13 floating factories were in a serviceable condition, while 8 factories and 39 whaleboats were lost. Even so, Norway could send 10 floating factories to the whaling grounds in the 1948/49 season, and Norway was responsible for slightly more than half of the total catch of 2.2 million barrels of oil.

The question of utilising the whale carcase as fully and rationally as possible has come more and more to the foreground, because of the reduction in whale stock. In the research laboratories ashore, as well as with the expeditions, scientists work on the many problems involved: deep-freezing of whale meat, utilisation of the liver for vitamin products, extraction of insulin from the pancreas, and many other things. In particular, the problem of covering the deficit of fat in the diet of the world's population has turned the attention of experts to the rich source of supply provided by the whaling industry.

The Norwegian whaling expeditions have also carried out important geographical research work. Immense unexplored territories have been charted, partly from ship-borne aircraft, and the knowledge of these not easily accessible parts of our globe has been increased through their meteorological and oceanographic observations, which open up possibilities for a rational utilisation of the riches of Antarctic waters.

Of great importance is also the seal and walrus hunting in arctic waters during the summer months.

nected with shore-based stations, which made them dependent on concessions.

Another revolutionary development was introduced in 1925, when the whaling company "Globus" of Sandefjord sent its floating whaling factory *Lancing* to Antarctic waters, equipped with a hauling slipway. With the help of this slipway they could haul the whale carcase on board to be cut up and sent directly down into the big boilers below deck. This new development converted whaling into a "floating industry" which carries on its production on the open sea all through the season without any shore connections. These floating factories are vessels of up to 25,000 tons deadweight, and cost from 25 to 30 million kroner (1,5 million pounds sterling), while the whaleboats which do the actual catching are now being built up to 500 gross tons with engines of 1,800 h.p. or more. A single factory can produce more

The automobile ferry links one road with another along the Western coast.

TRAVELLING IN NORWAY

NORWAY IS closely connected with both the Continent and Great Britain by a number of excellent traffic arteries. Whether travelling by air, by land or by water, a trip to Norway to-day is a pleasant experience, with comfortable accomodations and full of new, exciting impressions.

If one prefers travelling by land, trains from Paris, Amsterdam, Brussels or Zurich carry the tourist through Denmark and southern Sweden into Norway. Fine roads also lead from the Continent through southern Scandinavia. However, for many it will be more natural to use the excellent steamer connections between Norwegian ports and for instance Rotterdam, Amsterdam or Newcastle. Coming from the distant west, there are regular sailings with modern liners from New York to Bergen, Stavanger and Oslo. Finally, a number of airlines operate on practically daily schedules between the most important cities in Norway and the great European capitals and America.

However, whether proceeding by one means of transportation or another, Oslo or Bergen are the most commonly used ports of entry into Norway. Bergen is situated in the heart of the fjord districts of western Norway — the section which perhaps more than any other

has given Norway its world reputation as a tourist country. During the summer season, Bergen has daily connections with the great fjords by means of bus, steamer and railway, and good hotels are found everywhere in beautiful surroundings. From the western fjords, bus and rail transportation is available across the mountain plateaus and down into the broad, smiling valleys of eastern Norway.

From Oslo, the network of roads and railways spreads out to all parts of the country — through the valleys, across the mountains or along the coast — providing a number of different and varied routes by which to reach southern, western and northern Norway. Travelling by steamer along the Norwegian coast has a charm of its own, and the views of scenic beauty become ever more impressive as one proceeds northwards, reaching a magnificent and over-powering climax in the far north, where the Midnight Sun and North Cape are the great attractions of this fascinating fairy land.

Many prefer to see Norway from the deck of a great tourist liner, and the smaller Norwegian coastal steamers can hardly compete so far as comfort is concerned. However, if one seeks closer contact with the population and a more intimate understanding of what goes on in the country one will, nevertheless, prefer the smaller ships that put into innumerable little places along the coast, thus providing a rich and varied picture of the conditions under which the Norwegian people live and work. And the many new steamers that are being put into service along the coast satisfy all reasonable requirements as to comfort.

The Norwegian railways are not so rapid as the trains on the continent, but in a country like Norway, with its magnificent and ever-changing nature, one really needs more time for the trip. Big observation windows in the new, comfortable day coaches afford splendid opportunities for admiring the lovely countryside unfolding itself along the railway.

In a mountainous country such as Norway, staggering amounts are needed for the construction of railways, and it is only to be expected, therefore, that the rail net has not been developed so extensively. However, where rail transportation is not available, Norwegian construction workers and engineers have carved fantastic roads right into the mountainside. In the summer season, fine and comfortable busses operate daily along these routes, providing an even better opportunity than train travel for intimate contact with nature and the life of the people.

Norway has a number of first-class tourist and mountain hotels throughout the most important tourist districts of the country. There are, moreover, clean, well-appointed and moderately priced hotels all over the country, and in order to be classified as a hotel an establishment must satisfy strictly defined requirements as to comfort and service.

For those who want to live even cheaper and have an opportunity to become even more intimately acquainted with the nature of Norway and perhaps above all with the youth of Norway, there is a network of youth hostels that are open in the summer all over the country. In the mountain regions the Norwegian Tourist Association and local organizations maintain really excellent cabins, suitably spaced an easy day's march apart.

On one's first visit to Norway it is, perhaps, advisable to travel according to a pre-arranged itinerary, which has been drawn up by people who are familiar with the transportation facilities and hotel accomodations, thus ensuring satisfaction. The next time, however, one might want to strike out on one's own, and there are few other countries that lend themselves better to adventurous exploring than Norway, with its unlimited range of ever-changing scenic beauty, the many different types among the population, and the varying ways of life.

Norway from the Air.

Few countries in the world need a highly developed system of air transportation more than Norway. With its tremendous distances and the mountainous terrain,

Norway has always been faced with the problem of communication and transportation between the scattered communities of the far-flung nation.

Already before the Second World War Norway had built up a net-work of both domestic and European air communications. The operations were, however, interrupted by the German occupation in 1940.

Since the liberation in 1945, the Government and private interests have co-operated in the rebuilding of the Norwegian Air Lines. Thanks to the careful preparations made by the Norwegian Government in London during the war, it was possible — within a short period — not only to re-establish the old net-work, but in fact to extend it considerably, with lines now covering the whole of Scandinavia and most countries of Western Europe.

At the same time the old idea of establishing inter-Scandinavian co-operation in civil aviation ripened, and on August 1, 1946, the three Scandinavian countries, Denmark, Norway and Sweden, merged their national air line operations on the service to North and South America.

During the first year of joint operation, this consolidated Scandinavian air lines — operating under the name of Scandinavian Airlines System (SAS) — had become the leading European air carrier on the North Atlantic run, flying more passengers across the North Atlantic than any other European line. The success prompted the three parent companies to co-ordinate their other activites too, and since April, 1948, the Scandinavian Airlines System has had regular air service to four different continents, and to-day maintains one of the biggest net-works on the European continent.

Flying in Norway is to-day recognized as the quickest means of bringing mail, civil servants, business men and the like to the most remote places throughout the nation. It has also developed into one of our finest tourist attractions.

The flight to the Land of the Midnight Sun, for instance, which is operated by large four-engined flying boats, has become one of the most popular tourist runs in the whole world. Every summer thousands of foreign tourists, mostly American and British, enjoy this unique air service. Within six to seven hours the visitor to Norway can travel from Oslo to Tromsø, the capital of the Arctic, flying above some of the most beautiful and fascinating scenery, with a view of the deep fjords, the thousands of islands, the waterfalls, glaciers and rugged mountains, and — to the west — the endless Atlantic Ocean, with the horizon now and then broken by chains of mountains and snow-covered islands.

The Norwegians have endeavored to bring into aviation the same spirit which has always predominated in Norwegian shipping. We feel, indeed, that shipping and aviation have much in common, and it is our aim and

One of the large four-engined flying boats above the Lofoten Islands.

*One of the first-class hotels which are found in the regions offering
ideal skiing and magnificent scenery.*

ambition to build aviation on the old traditions of shipping, putting all our efforts not only into conquering the
air, but into making it the broad highway to and throughout Scandinavia.

Motoring.

There are first-rate tourist steamers connecting Newcastle—Oslo, Newcastle—Bergen/Stavanger, Antwerp—
Oslo, Rotterdam/Amsterdam—Bergen, Hamburg—Oslo,
and from Denmark: Copenhagen—Oslo and Fredrikshavn—Oslo. Special ferries for motorcars and passengers
operate between Hirtshals—Kristiansand, Fredrikshavn—
Larvik and Grenå—Arendal.

Freight rates for cars to Norway are very moderate,
lower, actually, than the rates for crossing the English
Channel. When a car is shipped by the same steamer
carrying the owner and his party, the freight rates are
reduced. This is so even when the passengers travel by
Norwegian airlines, forwarding their car by a Norwegian steamship line.

In addition to the steamer connections mentioned
above there is the main highway from Western Europe,
through Northern Germany, across the Danish Islands
and Southern Sweden to Oslo. From all parts of Sweden
a number of good roads lead to Norway.

Motorists are well received in Norway. All foreign
tourists are exempt from taxes (a road tax is included in
the gasoline price). The sale of gasoline is unrationed.

Motorists receive such touring information, advice
and other assistance as they may desire through the two
Automobile Associations, which are affiliated with similar clubs and international organizations for the promotion of automobile touring. Information is also given by
tourist and travel bureaus.

Oslo, the Capital of Norway, is the great natural center of motor-tourist traffic and the point of departure
for most of the main routes. Other centers or starting
points are the shipping ports of Bergen, Stavanger, Kristiansand, Larvik, Arendal and Trondheim.

Here are some of the main motoring routes:

1. *The coastal road Oslo—Stavanger (about 400 miles).*
On both shores of the Oslofjord and along the southern
coast you will find the Norwegian Riviera, where the
climate is mild, the spring early, the summer warm and
the autumn late. Scattered along the fjords and on the
numerous islands, in a setting of fertile and delightful
countryside, there are idyllic coastal towns, summer
resorts and bathing beaches.

Westward from Kristiansand the road runs over
wooded hills and highland moors, from one valley to
another, until it reaches the mighty plains of Jæren and
the North Sea with the airport of Sola and the city of

94

Famous among the road constructions of Western Norway is the "Trollstegveien" in Romsdal.

The Svinesund bridge on the Swedish border is the main entrance for car tourists from the Continent.

Stavanger. From Stavanger modern ferries for motorcars operate northwards to Haugesund and the Ryfylkefjords, and from these points roads carry you on to Hardanger and the city of Bergen.

From Oslo and Eastern Norway a number of roads run across the magnificent mountain ranges and plateaus of Central Norway and down to the famous and beautiful fjords of the West Coast, with the city of Bergen as the natural center.

2. *The southern-most of these roads* passes through the lovely valleys of Telemark, the original home of the ski sport, with lakes, rivers and waterfalls; over the mountains of Haukeli with a breath-taking view of the mountain ranges, and down the steep hills descending into the valley of Røldal. Here the road branches off to the fjords of Ryfylke and the city of Haugesund, and — running past the imposing waterfall of Låtefoss — to the industrial center of Odda, which is situated at the head of the Sørfjord, a branch of the beautiful Hardangerfjord, along shores of which are some of the most fertile fruit districts in Norway.

3. *The shortest road from Oslo to Bergen* runs through the valleys of Hallingdal or Numedal to Geilo and Haugastøl — centers for winter sports and summer hiking in the mountains — continuing across the magnificent mountain plateau of Hardangervidda and down the famous serpentine road of the Måbødal valley. Here you pass the great waterfall of Vøringfoss (about 600 feet high), and finally reach Eidfjord, another branch of

the Hardangerfjord. At Kinsarvik a modern ferry carries you across the fjord to Kvandal, where the road continues through the wild, narrow pass Tokagjelet to Bergen.

A branch of this road leads from Kvandal to Voss and — passing the Stalheim Hotel, which is perched on the cliffs of the steep and celebrated Stalheim pass — continues down to Gudvangen on the beautiful and narrow Nærøfjord, a branch of the great Sognefjord, the longest and deepest fjord in Norway, nearly 100 miles in length.

A net of modern car ferries operates between the chief road centers of Sognefjord, and travelling in this district, with its wonderful, everchanging scenery, is indeed a memorable experience.

Among the points of particular tourist interest in Sogn are Vadheim, Høyanger (a great industrial center) and Balestrand, all connected by roads leading northward to Sunnfjord and Nordfjord with the world-famous fjord sceneries of Olden, Loen and Stryn. From Stryn the road continues eastward across the mountain range and down into the valley of Gudbrandsdalen.

Leikanger and Kaupanger are starting points of the Sognefjell Road, which runs across the highest mountain pass in Norway (4,800 feet above sea level), through the wild and rugged mountains of Jotunheimen and down into the valley of Gudbrandsdalen (see below).

4. *From Lærdal*, at the eastern end of Sognefjord, another road leads up to the Lærdal valley (famous for its salmon fishing), across the mountain of Filefjell and

A road in one of the valleys of Sunnmøre.

down through the lang and beautiful Valdres valley to Fagernes. From Fagernes a number of different roads run south-east to the districts around the great lakes of Randsfjord and Tyrifjord and further on to Oslo.

From Årdal (a new industrial center), a serpentine road winds up the mountainside to a height of 3,000 feet, passing the Tyin lake to join the Filefjell Road. A branch of this road leads to the mountain lake of Bygdin.

5. *The great highway connecting Oslo—Trondheim* skirts the biggest lake in Norway, Mjøsa, which is surrounded by fertile farming districts, and passes through the cities of Hamar and Lillehammer. Lillehammer is a great tourist center, especially noted for winter sports and skiing.

From Lillehammer the highway continues up through the broad and beautiful valley of Gudbrandsdalen to Dombås, branching off into a number of side roads that lead up to mountain hotels on both sides of the valley.

From Dombås the road climbs to a height of 3,000 feet across the great mountain plateau of Dovre, and winds down the wild valley of Drivdal to Opdal (noted tourist center), and on to Trondheim, Norway's third city and ancient capital of the Middle Ages, with its beautiful Gothic Cathedral, the Technical College, a fine harbour. Trondheim is a natural communications-center, the point of departure for all traffic northward to the Land of the Midnight Sun.

From the Oslo—Trondheim highway a number of roads branch off to the fjords of Møre and Romsdal:

From Otta to Nordfjord with Stryn, Loen and Olden, and to the great tourist attraction, the Geirangerfjord, with ferry connections to the towns of Ålesund and Molde. From Dombås down through the Romsdal valley, with the towering summits of Romsdalshorn and Trolltinder, the famous, winding Trollsteg road, and the lovely passage along the Romsdalsfjord to Ålesund, which is linked to Molde by ferry. From Opdal to Molde and Kristiansund N. through the Sunndal valley and along the rugged, mountainous Sunndalsfjord.

The shortest distance by car from Oslo to Trondheim is through the valley of Østerdalen, the longest in Norway. The road passes through the vast forest districts along both shores of the Glomma, the greatest river in Norway, which springs from the mountain lakes near the ancient mining town of Røros. At Tynset the road branches off to Kvikne (the birthplace of the poet Bjørnstjerne Bjørnson) and Støren, and on to Trondheim.

6. *The Midnight Sun Road to Northern Norway* is the connecting link between the North and the South, reaching all the way up to the Polar Sea, North Cape and eastward to the Russian frontier near Kirkenes. It is a road of fairy-tale scenery and colors, with fjords, mountains and valleys of extraordinary beauty, and daylight around the clock in the summer.

The distance from Trondheim to Kirkenes or Vardø is great — nearly 1,250 miles. In order to take in the most interesting and characteristic points along this route one should make plans for a two or three week's trip.

The first part of the trip might be from Trondheim to Bodø, a distance of some 480 miles. Here you travel through the sweeping, fertile valleys and wooded hills of the inner Trondheimsfjord, the vast forests of the Namdal valley, past magnificent waterfalls up to the Majavatn lake, which is ringed by snow-capped mountains, and down the Vefsen valley to Mosjøen.

It is a beautiful drive along the Ranfjord, with a view of the great, glittering glacier Svartisen (The Black Ice) in the background, and up the Dunderland valley, over the mountains of Saltfjellene (here you cross the Arctic Circle) where the road reaches a height of 2,100 feet, with mountain peaks on all sides. Descending into the valley of Saltdalen you drive along the Saltfjord to the city of Bodø, with a view to the south of tremendous snow-capped mountain ranges. Here you have the world-famous Maelstrom, where great masses of water stream in and out with the lake water.

The second stage of the road carries you from Bodø (Fauske) to Narvik, a distance of about 130 miles. Four different ferries take you across the narrow fjords that cut deeply into the country. The scenery here is beautiful, especially where the view opens to the great Vestfjord with the strange and varying colors of the mountain wall of Lofoten. The city of Narvik is connected with Sweden by railway, and is the most important port of export for Swedish iron ore.

Leaving Narvik by ferry, you embark on the third stage of this great northern road, travelling some 150 miles through the Troms inland up to Lyngenfjord. Here beautiful mountain scenery alternates with sweeping valleys and forests, sometimes calling to mind the countryside of southeastern Norway. The various communities and fjords of the Troms inland are linked by a net of roads, and branch roads reach out to the city of Harstad

on the great island of Hinnøy, and northward to the city of Tromsø, the biggest town in Northern Norway (population 10,000) an the center of the Polar Sea traffic. Around Balsfjord and Lyngenfjord the scenery is particularly lovely. This section of the country is linked by road with Sweden and Finland. .

East of Lyngenfjord, the entire province of Finmark was destroyed by the Germans when they retreated in 1944. All houses were burned down, the cattle were killed, and the population was forced to evacuate. Reconstruction is in progress but not yet completed. There are no tourist hotels as yet, but several guest houses or inns have been built by the State. The living conditions in this section of Norway — an interesting and strange part of our country — are rather poor, and most of the scattered population make their homes along the fjords and coastal areas. The vast inland is the home of the Lapps and their reindeer.

The heads of the many great fjords that cut into the country from the North — Altenfjord, Porsangerfjord, Laksefjord, Tanafjord, Varangerfjord — are linked by a net of roads. A branch road leads to Hammerfest, the northern-most town in Europe, and other roads proceed to the Finnish border.

The distance from Lyngenfjord to the towns of Vadsø and Vardø is nearly 500 miles, and about the same to Kirkenes, the mining town near the Russian border, which has been closed since the war.

The Bergen — Oslo railway.

Many of the railways in Norway give the traveller a rich and varied impression of the country. Most of them start from Oslo, following the long, winding valleys into the interior. In southern Norway, there are two railways traversing the mountains above the timber-line: The Oslo—Trondheim railway, and the Bergen—Oslo railway.

The Bergen—Oslo railway is justly considered one of the most magnificent mountain railways in Europe. From the ocean and deep fjords of the west to the broad, smiling valleys and rolling fields of the east — broken only by the harsh nakedness, the snow, ice and rock of the intervening mountain ranges, the railway gives a cross-section view of the scenery of Norway and, in a variety of ever-changing pictures, the conditions under which her people live and work.

Rising slowly from sea-level at *Bergen*, the railways runs some 60 miles in land to the open, agricultural district of *Voss*, which is an important tourist

An example of modern road construction in the fjord district. A two-way tunnel.

A rotating snow-plough at work clearing the railway line at Finse.

center. From Voss, roads affording views of unusual beauty lead to *Ulvik* and *Eide* in *Hardanger*, and via *Stalheim* and its steep, rocky pass down into *Sogn*.

Leaving Voss, the railway climbs steeply and passes through the 3 mile-long tunnel *Gravehalsen*, reaching *Myrdal Station* where an enrapturing view is obtained down the narrow, wild valley of *Flåm*. Here a serpentine road with numerous curves winds down the valley, running alongside of a branch of the railway which in parts has been carved right into the mountainside.

At Myrdal the "mountain adventure" begins — tunnels, overhead protection, rocks, waterfalls, lakes, snow, ice. The railway soon reaches its highest point, 4,267 feet above sea level, and shortly after we have *Finse Station*, 4,000 feet about sea level, with snow on its slopes and ice on the lake even at midsummer. Finse has a well-known tourist hotel.

Lying to the south and quite close is the snow-covered dome of *Hardangerjøkelen*, 6,232 feets high, and, to the north, the migthy, rocky wall of *Hallingskarvet*. The stations after Finse: *Haugastøl*, *Ustaoset* and *Geilo*, are also situated on the mountain plateau above the timber-line. Here are a number of hotels, among them some of the best known to tourists, and numerous ski cabins, mostly belonging to residents of Oslo and Bergen, are clustered around the stations. From Geilo the railway descends rapidly down into the valley of *Hallingdal*, and the mountain crossing is over. Continuing towards Oslo, the railway passes through broad, fertile valleys and wooded hill districts typical of eastern Norway.

The contrast in temperature, air and landscape between the barren world of rocks and ice on the mountain plateau, and the comparatively luxuriant scenery of Eastern Norway offers a striking illustration of the ever-varying character of life conditions in this country.

From a technical point of view the laying of the tracks presented formidable difficulties, and the railway has come to be looked upon as a masterpiece of engineering. Winter and summer alike, traffic proceeds smoothly and regularly, although considerable obstacles are encountered from snow. Winter storms are not to be treated lightly: the snowfall can be extremely heavy, and large masses of snow to a depth of 50 feet have been measured, frequently tightly packed into hard drifts by the fierce gales. As some protection against this hazard, particularly vulnerable sections of the railways for a total distance of some 60 miles across the mountains have been roofed and fenced in, and powerful rotating snowploughs have been procured to keep the tracks clear.

The total length of the railway is about 300 miles. Altogether, there are 179 tunnels having a total length of some 40 miles.

*A peasant wedding
in the old style
at Voss.*

*A varied scenery of mountains, lakes and glittering snow fields unfolds
before the traveller on the Bergen—Oslo railway.*

"The Seven Sisters", a famous waterfall in Geiranger.

REGIONAL DESCRIPTIONS

Now, we are going to take a journey right through the whole of Norway. We have divided the country into several parts, according to their geographical position. Starting our journey with a visit to Oslo, the capital city, we also get to know the surrounding districts. Then we go on, and take a trip to the broad, forested valleys of Eastern Norway, where the farms are large and the climate pleasant and dry. Further to the west, we visit Telemark and Setesdal, two large and important districts which belong neither to the west country nor to the east, and which lie between the mountain highlands and Sørlandet (the Southern Coast) which we come to next. Sørlandet, with its small, white houses and the innumerable islands with rich flora, is surely the most gentle part of an otherwise imposing country. From Sørlandet we take a trip up the Rogaland coast, the south-west "corner" of Norway, which leads to Vestlandet (Western Norway) with its long, narrow fjords, high and wild mountain regions and dazzling glaciers. After this coast of incomparable grandeur and beauty we give a description of the highland plateau and mountain districts which stretch right across the whole of Southern Norway. Leaving this region of

mountains and moors, we visit Trøndelag, the rich district to the north of the Dovre mountains. Trøndelag was the cultural center of Norway for many centuries, and in Trondheim is the cathedral where, still, Norway's Kings are crowned. Beyond Trøndelag lies Northern Norway, that long, narrow strip of country which ends at the North Cape, jutting straight out into the Arctic Sea.

Besides descriptions of the landscape, and giving the characteristics of each region, we have mentioned the means of livelihood which are most important in each particular part of the country.

Though this book is too modest a work to mention all the places well worth visiting, and though the pages are too few for all those pictures we could have wished to show you, we have tried to give as complete a picture as possible within a limited space. By looking at all the pictures consecutively, remembering that there were many others we would have liked to include, the reader will, we hope, get a fair impression of this beautiful country. And though our descriptions have had to be short, we hope that they will serve to stimulate the reader to find out more about this fairy-tale country of the North.

101

The waterfront of Oslo is dominated by the new City Hall.

OSLO AND ADJOINING DISTRICTS
Oslo with the Oslofjord.

FROM SKAGERAK the Oslofjord cuts some 60 miles northwards into the country. At the head of the fjord lies the capital city of *Oslo*. The approach to the city is exceptionally beautiful. Entering from the south, between the slender lines of the Færder Lighthouse on the left and the Torbjørn rocks on the right, the coast rises from the sea as a low, faint outline of hills; gradually towns and factories stand out from among the bare knolls and low, wooded slopes, and assume characteristic shapes and contours.

Horten, the naval base of the country, is situated on the western shore, and right across the fjord, close on the island of Jeløy, lies the industrial town of *Moss.* Continuing up the fjord one passes the small summer resorts of *Son* and *Hvidsten* to the east, and *Holmestrand* to the west. In the narrow sound that marks the entry to the inner fjord lies the old maritime town of *Drøbak,* small and picturesque with its many summer homes. Facing Drøbak is the island fortress of Oscarsborg. On April 9, 1940, a torpedo from this fortress sank the 10,000 ton German heavy cruiser "Blücher".

Emerging from the Drøbak narrows, the fjord opens into a wide basin with Nesodden rising tranquilly to the east. To the west are the islands, meadows and hills of Asker and Bærum. In the background are seen the characteristic wooded hilltops of Vardåsen, Skaugumåsen, Kolsås and — later — Holmenkollen, Tryvandsåsen and Grefsen. They all seem to stand guard over Oslo.

Oslo is one of the biggest cities in the world — in area. On January 1, 1948, the city was merged with the neighboring municipality of Aker, thus getting a total area of 175 sq.miles. After the merger, Oslo has miles of forest land, smiling lakes and rivers with roaring rapids right within the city limits! The present population is approximately 450,000.

Oslo was founded by King Harald Hårdråde 900 years ago. King Christian IV rebuilt the city in 1624 and moved it a little farther west, renaming it Christiania. However, in 1925 the original name of Oslo was restored.

Lying at the head of a fjord which is practically free from ice, with a spacious, sheltered harbour, with fine agricultural districts in its immediate neighborhood, and with excellent railway and road connections to other parts of the country, Oslo's geographical location is in-

The Royal Palace in Oslo.

deed a favorable one. More than half of all imports into Norway pass through Oslo, with a total annual value of 1,200 million kroner. Exports run into more than 200 million kroner.

As the residential city of the Royal Family, the seat of the Government and the Parliament ("Stortinget"), as well as the center of the federal administration in general, Oslo is the first city of the land and — naturally enough — the cultural center of the nation. Here we have the University of Oslo, founded in 1811, the University Library with some 1,000,000 volumes, the Deichman Library, a number of scientific foundations, and

schools of every kind. Oslo furthermore, is the Academy of Science, the Nobel Foundation, and a number of museums.

Karl Johansgate is the main street, running through the center of the city from the Central Railway Station up to the Royal Palace. The street is named after the builder of the Palace, Karl Johan, King of Sweden and Norway 1814—44, formerly a general in the French Revolution by the name of Marshal Bernadotte. An equestrian statue of Karl Johan stands before the Palace. The University, the National Theater and the Parliament are all located on this street.

The Royal family saluting the school children's procession on Norway's Constitution Day, May 17th.

The Monolith, high point of the Vigeland Sculpture Park.

A few years ago a number of new university buildings were constructed at Blindern, outside the old city limits.

Otherwise, the most characteristic building in Oslo is, perhaps, the ancient Akershus Castle, which dates back to the 13th Century and which in olden days was both the royal residence and the fortress of the city. In recent years the castle has been used by the State and the Municipality as the place of official entertainment.

Not far from this medieval castle is the new City Hall. With its tall center section and the two mighty towers its stands out dominantly in the skyline of the city, and can be seen from far down the fjord. Its architectural style is strongly influenced by the functionalistic tendencies of the 20th Century. Both inside and out the City Hall has been adorned and decorated with the works of outstanding Norwegian artists. The total cost is over 30 million kroner.

Other great buildings of recent date are the Telegraph Building, the offices of the Municipal Lighting Company, the Broadcasting House and Ulleval Municipal Hospital, the biggest in Scandinavia.

Some of the most beautiful parts of the city are found in the northern section, where great areas are covered with modern housing projects. Around the actual heart of the city there is a wide belt of villas and residences.

Ten minutes by street-car from the center of the city is the Frogner Park with the famous Vigeland sculptures. This ambitious project which, incidentally, has been a matter of great controvercy among art connoisseurs, was begun eighteen years ago, but has not yet been completed. It includes Vigeland's greatest compositions and an almost unbelievable number of sculptural works. A fifty-five foot high obelisk, the Monolith, forms the center of the sculpture park.

Near the Frogner Park is the Vigeland Museum, the sculptor's former studio which was erected for him by the City of Oslo. A number of Vigeland's works are found here. (See page 39, "Sculpture").

In the Frogner Park is the Oslo Municipal Museum, which is housed in a great, 150 year old manor house.

Farther south, on the peninsula of Bygdøy, lies the Norwegian Folk Museum with its magnificent collections of some 80,000 objects, depicting the life and cultural history of the Norwegian peasant for over a thousand years. No visitor to Oslo should fail to make a trip to this truly unique museum. At Bygdøy are also found the three world-famous Viking ships, the Oseberg Ship, the Gokstad Ship and the Tune Ship. These ships date back to the time of the Vikings (about 800 A.D.), and were found at the entrance to the Oslofjord. In connection with the Folk Museum we have the Norwegian Maritime Museum, which gives the visitor a good picture of Norway as a maritime nation. There is, furthermore, the Fram Building with the polar vessel "Fram", which was used by Fridtjof Nansen and Roald Amund-

One of the reptile groups flanking the bridge in the Frogner Park.

sen. This ship has been farther south and north than any other vessel in the world. (See "Exploration".)

King Haakon has a lovely summer residence at Bygdøy —this charming "island" which was presented by a Norwegian king to his queen on their wedding morn some 700 years ago. Here is also the small "Oscarshall" palace built by king Oscar I a hundred years ago.

At Frognerseteren, six miles from Oslo by suburban electric railway, the world's first Ski Museum was opened in 1922. Here the visitor will find everything connected with the national sport of Norway, one of the most interesting items being skis nearly 2500 years old. These skis were found many years ago in a swamp.

But the center of Oslo, too, has much of interest to offer the visitor in the way of museums. One of the most important is the Museum of History, with particular emphasis on the rich collection of medieval church art. In this museum are also exhibited all the objects that were found buried in the Oseberg Ship. Then there is the Museum of Applied arts, and the National Art Gallery with a highly representative collection of Norwegian paintings.

Sunset on the inner Oslo fjord.

Life at one of the bathing beaches near Oslo.

Norderhov Church on Lake Tyrifjord.

The districts north of Oslo.

When the people of Oslo seek recreation, they usually go to the districts north of the city—except, perhaps, in the hottest time of the summer.

Nordmarka is a mighty area of forest land that stretches northwards for a distance of nearly 30 miles. The southernmost part is Voksenkollen, only a half hour by electric suburban railway from the center of Oslo.

Here we have a natural wilderness with hills and ridges up to 2,000 feet high, and a multitude of little lakes. No public roads traverse these forests, and there is only a scattering of small houses and farms inhabited by lumbermen, and a few ski cabins. The area can only be compared with a great virgin national park.

This is the favorite haunt of the people of Oslo. In the summer they go for walks and hikes on foot, in the winter on long ski trips. Nordmarka is especially popular in the winter, when young and old alike go up to into the hills by the electric railway, "Holmenkollbanen", put on their skis and follow the countless ski trails through the forests. There is probably no other area in the world criss-crossed by so many ski trails. A great many of the people living in Oslo consider Nordmarka the greatest asset connected with their life in the city.

At the northwestern end of Nordmarka the mountain ridges plunge precipitously down towards the smiling and fertile agricultural district of *Ringerike*, which lies between the inland lakes of Tyrifjord and Randsfjord. Skirting the eastern shore of Tyrifjord is the main road from Oslo. The drive by car from Oslo is a lovely trip, with a beautiful view of the Tyrifjord from a point high up in the mountainside where the road emerges through a narrow pass.

Passing the old inn at Sundvolden (first mentioned in 1648), the road crosses the shallow sound at the head of Steinsfjord with Sundøya Restaurant, and continues northwards through the level meadows of Ringerike to the town of *Hønefoss*. A primitive funicular leads from Sundvollen up to Krokkleiva, where there is a look-out called "The King's View" with a wonderful vista. 1,500 —1,800 feet below, the fields, woods and lakes of this sweeping countryside stretch like a bright, variegated patchwork quilt, beyond which wooded ridges and mountain-tops fade away into the azure of the distant horizon.

On a point in the Tyrifjord lies the ancient, romantic stone church of Bønsnes, with a lovely interior. According to legend the church was built by St. Olav, who was King of Norway around the year 1,000. Farther north lie the church and rectory of Norderhov. The rectory is known from an episode in the war of 1716 against Sweden, when the pastor's wife, Anna Colbjørnsdatter, lured the Swedes into a trap.

The town of Hønefoss (population 3,500) is situated where the rivers of Randselv and Ådalselva meet. The name is taken from the waterfall of Hønefoss which has a drop of 60 feet. A number of factories located on the banks of the river get their power from this waterfall.

Hadeland is the rich agricultural district that borders on the northeastern part of Nordmarka. It is a pleasant country in all seasons, but perhaps most beautiful in the tints of the autumn when the golden, regular fields alternate with deep-green meadows and patches of black, ploughed earth. A splendid panorama is obtained from the hilltops in the east—Hvalbykampen (2,300 feet high) and Brandbukampen (1,600 feet). In winter, Hadeland offers an open and easy terrain for ski-ing.

This white-clad, virgin woodland is within an hour's journey from the center of Oslo.

The districts of Østfold and Vestfold.

The two counties on the eastern and western shores of the Oslofjord, Østfold and Vestfold, have some of the best farm land in Norway, and here we find several of the oldest manor houses in the country, rich in tradition. The low-lying countryside is broken and luxuriant, with many bights and coves along the fjord, making the landscape vivid and richly varied.

All the larger towns on the eastern shore of the Oslofjord are situated on or near a river estuary. These waterways cut through dense forest areas, and the chief industries of these parts are, therefore, naturally identified with the forest. The export of pulp and paper products is an important part of the economy of the districts.

The border town of *Halden* is situated on the estuary of the river Tista, which empties into Iddefjorden. The town (about 9,500 inhabitants) has played an important part in the history of the country, and it was during the siege of the Fredriksten fortress that King Carl XII of Sweden was killed in 1718.

Sarpsborg (population 13,000) lies about 10 miles from the mouth of the river Glomma, which here forms an impressive waterfall, Sarpsfossen. Here we have A/S Borregaard, the biggest Norwegian company in the pulp and paper industry and one of the foremost of its kind in Scandinavia. A/S Hafslund supplies electric energy to large areas of Eastern Norway, and is a producer of carbide and ferro-silicium.

Fredrikstad is situated on the estuary of the Glomma, Norway's longest river, in the most important lumber area of the country. The population is nearly 25,000. It is an important commercial town with a fine harbour and a big shipyard. Fredrikstad was founded in 1567, and is the only fortress town in Norway. In the oldest section many of the old buildings are still standing, lending to the town an air of bygone days.

Moss (founded in 1720) has some 17,500 inhabitants. As in all the other towns of Østfold, the manufacturing industries are the most important, especially flour mills and canning factories.

An hour's trip from Oslo, on the western side of the fjord, lies *Drammen*, a town of about 27,000 inhabitants. The town is situated on both shores of Dramselva near

108

The ancient church at Borre in Vestfold.

the river mouth. The districts along the river have many industries, and the town is an important shipping port. There are a number of lovely and fairly large farms in the neighborhood, and in the valley of Lierdalen gardening and truck farming are an important means of livelihood.

Drammen's nearest neighbor to the west is *Holmestrand*, a picturesque little town. Here we have a large aluminium plant. Farther west is *Tønsberg* (about 19,000 inhabitants), the oldest commercial and shipping town in Norway (founded in 870), and one of the most important in the country. The modern whaling industry has made this town into a prosperous community. On top of "Slottsfjellet" ("The Castle Mountain") are found ruins of the ancient fortress Tunsberghus, and a lookout tower 190 feet high.

Sandefjord, south of Tønsberg, was known for its lumber export as early as 1400 A. D. The population is about 15,000. The town is, one might say, the capital of modern whaling, and as such plays an important part in Norwegian trade and industry. Vestfold has always been the centre of the whaling industry, which has brought Norway more than one hundred million pounds in foreign exchange from 1905 to the outbreak of World War II. Sandefjord has the only whaling museum in the world.

Larvik (population 10,000) has the only beech forest in the country, in the vicinity of which lie the Farris Baths. Larvik became a municipal township in 1671. In the old feudal residence "Herregården", which was erected in 1679, there is a museum. The town is situated on a lovely spot where the rivers Numedalslågen and Farriselva empty into the sea.

The railway Vestfoldbanen proceeds along the idyllic lake Farrisvannet to the end station of *Eidanger*, where there is a beautiful 12th century wooden church.

From Eidanger a branch of the railway runs to *Brevik*, a small town with a big cement factory just outside the town limits.

Porsgrunn (9,000 inhabitants) is situated on both shores of Skienselva where this river empties into Frierfjorden. The only porcelain factory in the country is located here. Not far from the town, in Eidanger, we have Herøya with the great factories of Norsk Hydro.

Sandefjord, the home port of many whaling expeditions.

The market place in Tønsberg.

*Drammen was the first town
to erect a monument to
a great skier, Thorleif Haug.*

*The ancient fortress of Fredriksten
dominates Halden.*

Heavily wooded hills alternate with extensive fields along the shores of Lake Mjøsa.

LAKE MJØSA

M J ø s a, Norway's greatest lake, covers an area of 138.8 sq. miles. It stretches in a south-east to north-west direction for a distance of about 60 miles, converging to the north and south and reaching a maximum width of about 10 miles. The surface of the lake is 400 feet above sea level, and its greatest depth is 1,450 feet. Thus, in some places, the bottom is about 1,050 feet below sea level.

The great agricultural districts on both shores of Mjøsa (Hedmark and Ringsaker in the east, and Toten and Biri in the west) are among the best and most fertile in the land. Dotted across the gently undulating countryside and set in a frame of deep-green forests, are large farms with extensive grain and potato fields.

The entire district is encircled by heavily wooded hills.

To the south, on the west bank of the lake, the mountain of Skreia rises to a height of 2,500 feet, from the top of which a beautiful view may be had of the surrounding countryside. Where the Mjøsa is at its widest lies the delightful island of Helgøya—the Pearl of Mjøsa—with the historically famous Hovindsholm estate on its southern point.

The great river of Gudbrandsdalslågen empties into Mjøsa at the northern end, and to the south the river Vorma issues forth to become a tributary to the Glomma. Not far below the exit of the Vorma is the town of *Eidsvoll*, with the historical building where the Norwegian Constituant Assembly met in 1814 to draft and sanction the liberal Constitution of the country.

The modest manor house of Eidsvoll was the cradle of Norway's Constitution.

On the shores of the Mjøsa are the three small towns of the district: *Hamar* to the east, *Gjøvik* to the west and *Lillehammer* to the north. Situated prominently on the slopes that rise gently away from the smiling lake, they bring emphasis to the luxuriant, colorful surroundings.

Hamar is an ancient town, 900 years old. When at the height of its prosperity in the Middle Ages, it was the official residence of the bishop, with a splendid cathedral of which only some picturesque ruins still remain just outside the town. It is the natural center of Hedmark County, and an important railway junction. One railway line runs north through the valley of Gudbrandsdalen to Trondheim, branching off at Dombås to Romsdal, and another line runs through the valley of Østerdalen to Trondheim.

On the western shore of the lake lies Gjøvik, "The white city on the Mjøsa", as it is frequently called. The town has some trade and industry, such as the Mustad factories, the world's biggest producers of fish hooks and one of the biggest producers of horsenails. A large, modern hotel is now being built.

Lillehammer is situated on the northern shore. The chief activities of this charming town are trade, industry and tourists. In a manner of speaking, Lillehammer is the capital of the Gudbrandsdalen valley, and the town has truly realized the obligations inherent in this position. Here, at "Maihaugen", are the Sandvig Collections ("De Sandvigske Samlinger"), together with the Norwegian Folk Museum at Bygdøy, our foremost museum depicting the life and culture of the Norwegian peasant of old (see page 23). The town is a highly popular re-

creation and sports center, with several fine tourist hotels situated in the hills above the town or up on the mountain plateau, only an hour's drive away. The famous author Sigrid Undset, winner of the Nobel Prize in 1924, had her home in Lillehammer.

The best view of Mjøsa and its environs is obtained from the lake steamer "Skibladner", from which—on a beautiful summer day or in the early autumn—these broad and friendly rural districts are seen clothed in their most attractive garb. In order to know Norway properly, one would do well to carry away the impressions of gentle Mjøsa and its charming surroundings; as a contrast to the wild and striking grandeur of the west and the north, and the picturesque, idyllic landscapes of the south, Mjøsa serves to complete a comprehensive picture of Norway today.

Ruins of the cathedral at Hamar.

The eroded cone of Tronfjell rises above the river scene at Alvdal.

THE VALLEYS OF EASTERN NORWAY
Østerdalen — The Glomma river districts.

WHEN TRAVELLING through the valley of *Øster-dalen*, one gains the impression of endless forests, with relatively few but well cultivated and densely populated open areas. The valley is, for the most part, narrow and confined, and the broader, more spacious regions are mainly found towards its northern end. Many of the farms are old, with buildings which are typical of the locality. The houses of the valley are characterised by their beautiful proportions, although the architecture is perhaps not so rich and extravagant as that of the districts around Lake Mjøsa.

The Østerdalen valley also includes the *Rendal* and *Trysil* valleys, which are the easternmost valleys in southern Norway. Østerdalen proper starts at Elverum and runs northwards for a distance of some 155 miles. Through the valley flows the river *Glomma*, the longest and largest river in Norway. The Elverum—Trondheim railway runs through the entire length of the valley. Lovely roads lead up through the side valleys, some of them continuing across the mountains. Not quite

halfway up the valley, at *Koppang*, the main road leaves the valley proper, bending eastwards into the Rendal valley, which it follows in a northerly direction, to return to the main valley, farther north at *Tynset*. Leaving this charming village, the road continues through *Kvikne*, past the rectory of Bjørgan, the birthplace of the great Norwegian poet Bjørnstjerne Bjørnson, and westvards to *Ulsberg* on the Dovre valley.

At *Atna* (19 miles north of Koppang) a beautiful but in places narrow road runs westwards past *Sollia*, through the foothills of the wild and lovely mountain region of *Rondane*, with its magnificent peaks more than 6,000 feet high, and thence to *Folldal*. The main highway through Folldal branches off from Østerdalen farther north at *Alvdal*, and proceeds to Hjerkinn on the mountain plateau of Dovre. Rising immediately to the north of Alvdal is the grey, cone-shaped summit of *Tronfjell* (Tron), the highest peak of the Valley (5,500 feet). Near the watershed at the northern end of Østerdalen is the picturesque copper-mining village of *Røros*, with its quaint

Among the modest, grey timber houses of Røros the church stands as a landmark of this ancient mining town.

old houses and a venerable church. The village dates back to the 17th Century. Life in the mines has been masterfully portrayed by the author Johan Falkberget, who himself worked there in his early youth.

To the east and west of Østerdalen and Rendalen are great mountain plateaus, moors and pastures interspersed with ravines and small, inhabited valleys, reaching as far east as Lake *Femundsjø* near the Swedish border.

Tranquil-looking mountains rise from the moors to heights of nearly 6,000 feet, chief among them being *Rendals-Sølen* to the east, and *Stor-Sølen* to the west.

There are no towns, in the administrative sense, in the Østerdalen regions, but *Elverum*, a dense and populous settlement at the southern extreme of the valley (and 18 miles northeast of Hamar), has every appearance of a town. Here stands the Glomdals Museum with its excellent collections depicting the life in the valley in bygone days. (See illustration page 23.) On April 9, 1940, the King, the Parliament and the Government came to Elverum in their flight from the Germans, and that same evening the Parliament held its final session on Norwegian soil—until it met again after the liberation.

South of Elverum, the Glomma flows through *Solør* and the counties of *Akershus and Østfold*, finally emp-

tying into the sea at Fredrikstad. The total length of the Glomma is 375 miles. Below the small town of *Kongsvinger*, the flow of the river is generally smooth and steady, but as one proceeds northwards long stretches of rapids and a number of large falls are encountered. The twenty larger waterfalls along the Glomma represent a total of $\frac{1}{2}$ million H.P., about half of which has been developed. Among the more important power stations Vammafoss, Sarpsfoss and Mørkfoss-Solbergfoss are worthy of mention.

The river, particularly in its upper reaches, is well stocked with fish, including trout, grayling, pike, turbot, perch and many other species.

Gudbrandsdal.

Next to Østerdal, the Gudbrandsdal valley is the longest in Norway. It runs in a north-westerly direction for a distance of about 87 miles from *Lillehammer* (at the north end of Lake Mjøsa) in the south, to *Dombås*, where it merges into the highland valley of *Lesja* and the Dovre plateau.

The valley is narrow, its sides being steep but sparsely covered with trees, and its hillsides rise steadily from

360 feet to about 2,000 feet. The river *Lågen* (Gudbrandsdalslågen) runs through the whole length of the valley. The melting mountain snow, which finds its way into Lågen through the many lakes and streams of *Jotunheimen*, gives to the river below Otta an amazing green colour which is largely responsible for the particular charm and beauty of this valley.

Traffic between East Norway and Trøndelag has from time immemorial followed this valley, the districts of which have been cultivated and inhabited from the most ancient times. On some of the farms still live the descendants of old chieftain families whose ancestors can be traced back to the earliest history of Norway. Evidence of a by-gone might and tradition can be seen in the fine old log houses: Bjølstad at *Heidal*, Stei and Tofte at *Fron*, Sandbu at *Vågå*, and Harildstad at *Kvikne*; and the ancient timber- and "stave-churches" to be found at *Ringebu*, *Nord-Fron*, *Vågå*, *Lom*, and *Dovre* also speak of ancient culture and prosperity.

At *Maihaugen*, Lillehammer, is the well-known *Sandvig Collection* of houses and churches, complete with furniture and effects. This collection is taken from, and illustrative of, all parts of the valley. A description of the Collection is found elsewhere in this book.

The railway to Dombås also runs through the valley. At Dombås one line branches off westward and continues through Lesja and Romsdal to *Åndalsnes* in the Romsdalsfjord, while the Dovre line, winding up the Dovre mountains, proceeds northwards to Trondheim.

A number of deep, lateral arms leave the valley in a north-westerly direction and lead to the mountain moors in the west; starting in the South, they are: *Gausdal*, with Bjørnstjerne Bjørnson's farm *Aulestad*; the river

A veteran timber-floater.

Vinstra's valley *Kvikne*; that of the river Sjoa, *Heidal*; and that of Otta, *Vågå*, which continues into *Lom*, *Bøverdal* and *Skjåk* towards Jotunheimen, and across to the valleys and fjords of Nordfjord and Sunnmøre.

The most built-up areas in the valley are to be found around churches and railway stations. By-roads lead up to several mountain moors and highland hotels and some of them further into the adjoining mountains regions.

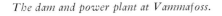

The dam and power plant at Vammafoss.

The river Gudbrandsdalslågen near Kvam.

Rising proudly from the highland plateau in the north of the valley are the *Rondane* mountains. Some of the peaks in this mighty range are higher than 6,000 feet, and their beautiful shapes make the mountains seem like gigantic fairy-tale castles on the plateau.

To the north-west are the rugged peaks of Jotunheimen, the most imposing mountain district of all Norway.

At *Hundorp* is to be found a monolith which is erected to the memory of King Olav the Saint. It was here that he, under dramatic circumstances, introduced Christianity to the people of the valley. A short distance up on the northern slopes near Vinstra is *Bakke*, a farm made famous by Ibsen's "Peer Gynt".

The Gudbrandsdal soil is extremely fertile, and agriculture is therefore the main industry. There are few manufacturing industries. Between Harpefoss and Vinstra a tremendous electric power station is being built inside the mountain; the water is carried 15 miles through tunnels, with a total drop of 1,470 feet.

The so-called Gudbrandsdal horse—a powerful, heavily built horse—is bred in the valley. The fine, rich goat cheese of the valley is also well-known.

Representative of the typical, longheaded Norwegian, the "Gudbrandsdøl"—or he who lives in the Gudbrandsdal Valley—shows the tradition of an old peasant culture.

Valdres.

The Valdres valley, through which the river *Begna* runs, starts where the river runs out into Lake *Sperillen*, and rises in a north-westerly direction towards *Filefjell* and the great mountains of the *Jotunheimen*. The southern part of the valley is a narrow, wooded pass where few people live. It widens out in the central region of *Aurdal*, where it is well cultivated and supports a comparatively large community. Dividing at *Fagernes*, the railway terminus, the valley sends out two arms. The eastern arm, *Østre Slidre*, leads to *Bygdin*, the southernmost of the lakes in Jotunheimen, while the western branch, *Vestre Slidre*, continues to Filefjell at a height of 3,200 feet, whence a very narrow valley leads to *Lærdal* in Sogn. There are many fine lakes in the upper valleys.

The scenery of Valdres is delightful and varied, and a number of tourist hotels have been built there. At several places the farms are built quite high up on the hillside. Fine stretches of pasture are found on the moors, with small communities of crofters' huts, and numerous lakes and streams with excellent fishing conditions abound. Motor boats ply the lakes *Tyin* and *Bygdin*, whence one has a superb view of the Jotunheimen. In the valley, sweet-smelling fields, silvery waters, sturdy

Lake Vangsmjøsa in Valdres.

forests and fine farms stand out against a background of snow-clad mountains.

Valdres is a long established favourite with tourists, and from ancient times the track crossing Filefjell has been a much-used route for traffic between Eastern and Western Norway.

Vassfaret, a narrow forest gully lying on the borders of Hallingdal, is one of the last retreats of the Norwegian bear.

Hallingdal.

The Oslo—Bergen railway line runs through the Hallingdal. This valley commences at *Gulsvik*, at the northern end of the long and straight lake *Krøderen*. The southern part of the valley is rather narrow but widens, at *Flå* and *Nes*, where it is more densely populated. At *Gol* the valley divides, the main branch to the west, and the other, *Hemsedal*, continuing in a north-westerly direction.

A main road passes through Hemsedal to *Lærdal* in *Sogn* in West Norway, reaching its highest point at the watershed (3,500 feet). The upper valley opens on to well cultivated ground with mountains to the north and south, the most imposing mountain being *Skogshorn*

(5,200 ft.) in the north. In the south can be seen a silver stripe down the sheer mountain face — the charming *Hornsfoss* waterfall.

Running west from Gol, the main valley is more varied in its aspect, with broad fields and fine farms often well up on the hillside. In many places the river flows along the bottom, forming large lakes.

An ancient "stave-church" once had its site in the pretty parish of Gol, but this church is now found in the Folkemuseum at Bygdøy (Oslo). Another stave-church is still standing, however, at *Torpe*, where it is flanked by a new church. A fine old church may also be seen on the northern shore of *Holsfjord*.

The valley proper ends at Hol, whence the railway and road climb sharply towards the mountains through the valley of *Ustedal*. They go side by side, passing through the tourist centres of *Geilo* and *Ustaoset*. Further west at the railway station *Haugastøl* (3,000 ft.) on the mountain plateau, they part company, the road taking a more southernly direction across the *Hardangervidda* highland moors, then descending abruptly to sea-level at *Eidfjord* in Hardanger.

Quick and alert, the "Hallingdøl" has from olden times been known as a clever fiddler and dancer (the Halling dance demanding a high degree of agility). Lately the national costume of the valley has again come into use

View from Hovet in Hallingdal towards Hallingskarvet.

— especially among the women — and it is a pretty sight to see them in their gaily coloured clothes against the deep green of the forest.

Numedal.

Numedal is one of the large valleys of East Norway, situated in the extreme south-west of this region. It starts at the mining town of *Kongsberg*, and rises steadily in a north-westerly direction to a point beyond *Nore*, where it ramifies.

Kongsberg was founded in 1624, close to a silver mine which then had just been sunk. The mine has been worked ever since with but few idle periods. One of the main pieces of baroque architecture in Norway, a beautiful church built 200 years ago, is to be found in the centre of the town. The interior of the church is especially beautiful and well worth a visit. The surrounding district is hilly and varied, and offers great opportunities for active sports, not least skiing. Many skiing champions of international renown have come from this town; the best known being the Ruud brothers.

Flowing through Numedal is *Lågen* (Numedalslågen), which comes from the large lakes on Hardangervidda, and flows out into the sea at *Larvik*. With its many lakes and falls, Lågen is one of the most important waterways for timber in Norway.

The lowest part of the valley passes through rather monotonous, wooded country where the population is rather scattered; in its middle section, however, in the neighbourhood of the long, narrow lakes, Kravikfjord and Norefjord, the landscape becomes more varied and large farms are seen on both sides, as well as evidences of an older settlement. Bordering the valley are steep mountains which attain a height of up to nearly 4,000 feet.

On the western slope of the valley, at *Nore*, lies a fine old church; and high up in the valley is the great state-owned hydro-electric power station of that name, which derives its waterpower from the rivers formed by *Tunhovdfjord* and *Pålsbufjord*. The railway which runs through Numedal has its terminus at Nore.

Opdal (Uvdal), the upper district of the valley, is a delightful, open highland parish surrounded by fine forest-slopes and lovely mountains. On the northern slope is an old stave-church and many ancient farm-buildings.

After leaving the valley proper, the main road continues across the highland in the north, and eventually reaches Geilo on the railway line from Bergen to Oslo.

The *Numedøl* in many respects resembles his half-brother, the *Hallingdøl*, and like him has long been in close touch with Hardanger, on the other side of the mountains. A generation ago, emigration from the valley to the United States of America was very great.

The stave-church of Heddal.

TELEMARK

TELEMARK is an inland district, lying between East-, South- and West-Norway, intersected and cut up by lakes and watercourses. The mountains are sharp and rocky, wooded slopes frequently attain a considerable height. Best known of its peaks is *Gausta* (Gaustafjell) which rises majestically to an altitude of 5,646 feet, clearly visible from a considerable distance on every side.

Well-tilled and well-planned rural districts and hamlets lie scattered along the lakes and valleys. For long, Telemark lay hidden and unknown. Cut-off, its people lived their own separate life and preserved their own methods of building, their own homecrafts, manners and customs, and their own dialect and national costume. The people lived well here with much fish in rivers and lakes, with plenty of game in the woods, and the grazing grounds were rich. The Telemark cow is one of the best and most select breeds of cattle in Norway. Whetstones and grindstones were obtainable in the mountains and, later, iron and copper deposits were discovered.

A few old buildings, often elaborately carved and with beautiful decorative paintings, still remain. Of notable old churches may be mentioned *Heddal's* stave-church, the largest in the country; that of *Eidsberg* at Dalen, and the stone churches of *Romenes* and *Bø*. Wood-carving,

Looking up the valley at Vinje in Western Telemark.

decorative painting and silversmith's work are handicrafts still carried on with taste and ability. In Norwegian peasant Art, the products of Telemark rank very high and the number of gifted artists is, perhaps, proportionately greater than in any other district. The collectors of folk music, fairy tales and ballads have made a rich harvest in these valleys, where medieval lore and age-old traditions remained alive afther they had disappeared in other parts of the country.

To-day, however, crossing and re-crossing this land of the "Telers" are roads and railways opening it to everyone. During the summer, steamboats or motorboats ply on several of the lakes *(Norsjå, Tinnsjø, Møsvatn* etc.). The watercourse from Skien westward to *Dalen* has been made navigable for steamer traffic by means of locks which obviate the many rapids and falls. The steamer journey along the Skien canal presents many a delightful landscape and several magnificent falls. The watercourses, particularly in the east, have been harnessed for industrial purposes. Factories, power-stations and towns now lie as close neighbours along the Skien watercourse and its tributaries Måne and Tinne, and along the river Skienselv. The river, between Tinnsjø and Heddalsvatn, has been harnessed for power purposes. Of recent origin is the industrial town of *Rjukan* (production of salpetre) taking its name from its mighty falls. With its imposing structures well placed amid the magnificent

scenery, Rjukan is picturesquely situated in the narrow, deep valley of Vestfjorddal, running at the foot of Gausta. True, in order to supply power the falls are directed into pipe-lines, but when the flow of water is heavy, Rjukanfoss can still rush and roar in all its ancient majesty and beauty.

Notodden at the head of Heddalsvatn, is the centre of the Norwegian salpetre industry. Important industries like paper, calcium carbide etc. are also situated in the town.

In the mouth of the Skien estuary are, from north, the towns *Skien, Porsgrunn, Brevik* and *Langesund.* Skien is the largest, having a population of about 10,000. It has an appreciable export trade mostly of timber, cellulose etc. and is the birthplace of Henrik Ibsen. Porsgrunn possesses important industrial plants, among them a renowned porcelain factory. Outside the town at Herøya are Norsk Hydro's great new plants producing fertilizers.

Further west on the coastline is the small picturesquely situated town Kragerø. This town is officially in Telemark, but it may be said that geographically it belongs rather more to Sørlandet.

The "Teledøls" are known as excellent ski-runners and it was people from Telemark who put fresh life into skiing as a sport and founded the modern school which was gradually adopted all over the world.

SUMMER NIGHT IN A VALLEY IN EAST NORWAY

From a painting by Christian Skredsvig

The costume of Setesdal still reveals its medieval origin.

SETESDAL

SETESDAL is the longest valley in South Norway. It is considered as commencing in south at the long, picturesque lake known as Byglandsfjorden, and it leads to the watershed of Haukeli in the north—a length of about 75 miles. The river *Otra* follows the valley and forms a number of delightful lakes and falls. South of Byglandsfjord the valley is known as *Torridal*, and runs straight south to *Kristiansand*, a distance of about 40 miles.

For a considerable period Setesdal was practically cut off from communication southward, and tracks in other directions crossed the desolate mountain moors. This so recently isolated and remote valley has therefore better preserved its dialect, its costumes, building methods, poetry and folk-tales than other valleys in the country. Fine old storehouses, mounted on wooden pillars and built of carved, age-old timber are still to be found on most of

the farms of long standing—notably at *Osa, Valle* and *Rygnestad*. The national costume is still worn both as daily and festival attire, in the latter case being particularly bright and pretty. To-day, as of old, youth assembles on the dancing-greens—small, specially prepared plots by the roadside.

The most beautiful spot in the district is the parish of Valle, about halfway up the valley, with fine old farms gathered about its church.

In the upper limits of the valley around *Bykle* (1,800 ft.), the coniferous forest ceases, but the birch woods continue for a considerable distance with solitary pine or fir trees in between. There are excellent lakes for fishing in these valleys.

There is a railway line from Kristiansand to *Byglandsfjord*, and a motoring road runs through the entire length

of the valley and crosses the highland moors in the north, connecting at *Haukeligrend* with the Telemark–Hardanger road. It only takes five hours with motor ferry from Hirtshals in Denmark to Kristiansand. Motoring tourists coming from the Continent therefore make much use of the Setesdal road, whether they are aiming for the east or west.

The steamer passage on the Byglandsfjord is picturesque, hamlets and well-managed farms being dotted along the pine-clad banks; no less than three churches are to be seen on the eastern shore. The valley converges towards the northern end of the lake, and, farther north, where it narrows considerably, its sides become steep and its population scanty.

The "Setesdøl" is an excellent silversmith, and his craft is plied and his work is sold at almost every farm throughout the valley.

Setesdal has long been a favourite with painters, and collectors of national songs and folk-tunes find that many are still preserved, verbally, by the people in the valley.

*A corner of one of the oldest **timber houses** in the valley, the famous "Rygnestadloftet".*

The valley bottom at Valle broadens into fertile plains.

The breakers of the Skagerak are constantly attacking the southern coastland.

SØRLANDET

Sørlandet (the south country) is the curve of the coast between Risør and Flekkefjord (west of Kristiansand)—a narrow strip of coastal country with the glens and heaths lying immediately within.

It is intersected and cut up by numerous small fjords and valleys. Along the coast is a wreath of tiny islands. There are many cosy, sheltered bays, many charming coastal towns, fishing hamlets and out-ports, besides delightful lakes and watercourses. On the heaths and along the rivers are many well-kept farms. Growing among the steep, but comparatively low hills and between the tilled fields are many kinds of trees. The vegetation is rich, the climate mild and genial. The soil, however, is shallow and requires much rain.

Steamer routes touch at the towns, the traffic on the smaller fjords and between the islands being carried by local vessels. The boats thread their way through lovely scenery which is constantly changing. At places the smaller steamboats creep through narrow sounds, the banks of which are so close that they tempt one to jump ashore! Roads skirt the coast and run up the valleys. Bus-services cover the whole district. The Sørlandsbanen railway line (Oslo–Stavanger) links the most important towns together, directly or by secondary lines.

Trips to the out-ports and fishing-hamlets are becoming increasingly popular. Nor should the woods and valleys be omitted — they also have their own particular charm.

Sørlandet is a paradise for yachting. Of its kind, there can be no better holiday than cruising down this smiling coast. The islands guard the coast-line, making the waters calm. There are innumerable natural harbours for anchoring.

Mostly situated among hills, the towns along Sørlandet's coast have a picturesque appearance. They mostly consist of small, white wooden houses in narrow, winding lanes, and a few stone houses in the more modern parts. Reckoning from the east, the towns are: Risør, Tvedestrand, Arendal, Grimstad, Lillesand, Kristiansand, Mandal, Farsund and Flekkefjord — towns which, together with Sørlandet generally, had their boom during the times of sailing frigates in the last century. The main towns are: *Arendal* (pop. 11,000), near the delightful island Tromøy. This town has always been in the forefront as a shipping town, and its present trade includes the export of timber, iron, copper and feldspar. *Kristiansand* (pop. 24,000), the chief town of Sørlandet, was founded in 1641. After a great and devastating fire, it

Brekkestø outside Lillesand is one of the many cosy sheltered harbours among the isles and skerries.

was replanned with broad and open streets, completely straight, which cut each other at right angles. Where the streets open up one can always see the ocean in one direction and the hills in the other. The principal exports are timber, nickel, copper, aluminium, feldspar and fish. Kristiansand is an important centre of communication.

The first town encountered west of Kristiansand is *Mandal*, the southernmost town in Norway. Through the town runs the river of that name, renowned for its salmon. It still has many examples of fine old architecture and is known as an idyllic summer resort with a sandy beach just outside the town.

Looking toward the Cathedral at Kristiansand.

A view of Lillesand, one of the typical white towns of Sørlandet.

*On the market-place of Stavanger, the statue of the great novelist
Alexander Kielland occupies a prominent place.*

ROGALAND

THE COUNTY OF ROGALAND is situated in the
south-west "corner" of the country, wedged in between
that part of Norway which is called Sørlandet (the
Southern country) and Vestlandet (the Western country). Rogaland comprises the coastal regions approximately from *Flekkefjord* in the south to *Haugesund*
in the north, including the countryside around the many
branches of *Boknfjorden*. All the towns lie on the coast,
the most important being *Egersund* in the south, *Sandnes, Stavanger* and *Haugesund* further north.

The towns.

Egersund is best known for its pottery-works, which
were founded a century ago. *Sandnes* is an industrial
town in rapid growth. The main industries are wool
mills, worsted spinneries, and bicycle factories. Ten miles north of Sandnes lies the chief town of the district,
Stavanger (pop. 50,000), on the southern shores of
Boknfjord. Stavanger is the fourth largest town in Norway. In the midst of beautiful surroundings lies the Stavanger Cathedral, one of Norway's most remarkable
structures from the Middle Ages. Interesting is also lake
Bredevannet, with the ancient market place, public park
and "Kongsgaard" — the one-time residence of the Ro-

man-Catholic bishops of Stavanger, and now a high
school. There is a permanent theatre and a museum.
Overlooking the market place there is a statue of Alexander Kielland, the novelist, who has given masterly de-
pictions of his native town. The canning industry is by
far the most important, canned fish and meat being exported in vast quantities each year, especially brisling
and herring. Stavanger probably exports more in this
field than any other port in the world.

Stavanger is the terminus of the so-called "Sørlandsbanen" railway line, linking Oslo with the most important towns along the coast of Southern Norway.

Immediately south-west of the city are the picturesque ruins of the old church of Sola, supposedly built in
the 11th century. The bay is a favourite bathingplace,
there is a golf course with unique surroundings, and good
tourist hotels. The Sola aerodrome is one of the most
important in northern Europe, with direct connections
to foreign and overseas countries.

On the island Karmøya, to the north of Stavanger,
are the two small townships of *Skudesneshavn* and *Ko-
pervik*. *Haugesund* (pop. 18,000) is situated on the
mainland near the northern extremity of the island. The
imposing town hall attracts special attention. Immediately outside the town is an obelisk — "Haraldstøtten"

Stavanger Cathedral.

Peasants of Rogaland.

Sand dunes at Jæren.

— raised in 1872 on the burial mound of King Harald Hårfagre to commemorate the millennium of the unification of Norway under one king. Haugesund is one of the largest ship-owning towns in the country and, moreover, it takes a very active part in the fishing industries of Norway.

Landscape.

The coastal plain between Egersund and Stavanger, about 35 miles long, is called *Jæren*. Curving towards the north-west and north, and rising gently from the sea, it forms the south-west coast of the country. As a bulwark against the waves are sand-dunes with shallow lakes here and there; the slightly undulating country rises slowly to low heather moors about 300 feet above sea level.

Jæren belongs to the earliest populated districts of Norway, and definite evidence has been found that people dwelt here as long as 6,000 years ago. Then their main occupation was fishing and hunting; to-day, however, a considerable part of the countryside is under cultivation, indeed, is on its way to become the granary of the country. With more and more good soil being brought under the plough, the district is assuming increasing importance. The farmers, who are known to be very industrious, have worked tremendously hard to rid their soil of the great masses of stone which are common to this part of the country. A delightful view of the northern part of the district is obtained from the hills of

Ullenhaug just to the south of Stavanger, or from *Synesvarden* (1,044 feet), Jæren's highest point.

Ryfylke is the fjord and the islands district lying immediately to the north of Stavanger, around the broad estuary of the Boknfjord. Cutting up the mountain masses, the fjords penetrate deeply into the country, and narrow valleys lead into the torn and broken mountain regions to the north-east and east (Ryfylkeheiene).

The many islands in the outer Boknfjord are fertile and densely populated. The vegetation along the fjord is luxuriant. Many rivers flow into the fjords, *Suldalslågen* in the north being a good salmon river.

The district has become a manufacturing centre of some importance, the modern chemical industries at *Sauda* being of particular interest. In the outlying parts of the district are rich herring and brisling fisheries.

There is much here that reminds one of Norway's ancient history. Well worth seeing is *Utstein* monastery with its beautiful stone church on Mosterøy, and the stave-church at Årdal.

A boat trip among the islands and fjords of Ryfylke reveals an ever changing, delightful scenery. The neighbourhoods of Vikedal, Nedstrand, Sauda and the wild-looking Lysefjord are notable tourist attractions. From Sand the main road follows the river Suldalslaagen to the lake *Suldalsvatn*. Here a ferry brings one to the north end of the lake, and a splendid road continues through Bratland to Hardanger and Telemark.

M/S "Stella Polaris" in Hjørundfjord, Sunnmøre.

WESTERN NORWAY

IN THE SOUTHERN PART of Norway the country is divided by a mighty mountain range which runs north—south. To the west of this range, between the mountains and the Atlantic Ocean, is found one of the loveliest and most remarkable tourist regions not only in Norway, but in the entire world.

Narrow, deep fjords penetrate far into the country, and from the shores the mountains rise almost vertically, the summits often being covered by everlasting snow. In spite of its wild ruggedness, the landscape is exceptionally luxuriant on account of the humid climate and the mild winter brought about by the Gulf Stream. The region is known as a rich fruit-growing district. From the almost innumerable fjords, steep and narrow valleys continue inland, frequently leading to icy-green mountain lakes or glaciers. Many of the rivers abound in fish such as salmon and trout.

Through the most important valleys roads have been constructed at great cost, and some of them also traverse the mountainous regions dividing Western and Eastern Norway. Tourists travelling by car have a choice of several different routes which give one a lasting impression of this truly magnificent scenery. But the tourist travelling by boat will also find it a memorable experience to take a trip through this network of glittering fjords

surrounded by gigantic mountains. The season is from June until the middle of September. In July the hotels are often over-crowded, and tourists who prefer to be independent of bookings, will do well to choose another time.

The towns of Western Norway are situated along the coast. Here are excellent harbours behind a string of countless islands that form a bulwark against the ocean. The chief means of livelihood are commerce, shipping, fishing and industry. Farther inland, at the heads of the fjords, are a number of smaller communities. A few great industrial plants have been erected in places where it has been found profitable to utilize the tremendous waterfalls of Western Norway. The population outside the towns earns its livelihood by fishing, farming and gardening.

Hardanger.

Hardanger has long been recognised as one of the most beautiful districts in Norway. Poets have sung its praise; and A. Tidemand's painting of a bridal procession on the fjord has also helped to make it widely known. The broad outer fjord is exquisite with its rich vegetation and stately farms, grouped round the church. Rising proudly from among its fellow-mountains is *Melderskin* (4,280 feet). On the southern bank of the fjord is the one-time

*Skjeggedalsfossen, a water-
fall in Hardanger (total
height 1,800 feet).*

*Rosendal, a baronial manor
built in the 17th century.*

In spring, the orchards of Hardanger are a cloud of blossom.

barony of *Rosendal*, formed by the fusion of a large number of estates under the powerful Osnes family. No fewer than 92 farms throughout Hardanger once belonged to this property, which was one of the rare cases of feudal domain in a country of independent freeholders. A considerable number of farms still belong to Rosendal, which was bequeathed to the University of Oslo on the death of the last head of the house. A short distance up the fjord is the beautiful seat of the family, a building of rough stone in an extensive park.

Slightly further inland, on the northern bank of the fjord, is the delightful spot *Norheimsund*, where an interesting motoring road continues westward to Trengereid and Bergen, and eastward to *Granvin* and *Ulvik*.

It is only in the districts of the inner fjord, however, that the real beauty of Hardanger unfolds. Here the fjord divides into several long, narrow arms, proceeding north, east and south.

Here the scenery is enchanting. The rich meadows and orchards, the forests and white-painted churches, the hotels and neat, well-kept farms, are crowned by imposing mountains. Of small townships and settlements may be mentioned *Utne, Eide* and *Ulvik* on the Eidfjord, and *Ullensvang* on the *Sørfjord*, where *Tyssedal, Eitrheim* and *Odda* have developed into large industrial and water-power centres.

Rising perpendicularly from the fjord to a height of more than 4,800 feet are mighty mountains in the north and east. To the south is the *Folgefonna glacier* (4,959 ft) and in the east is the steep wall of rock which supports the roof of the district, *Hardangervidda*. The bluish-green snow-mantle of *Hardangerjøkelen* is glimpsed in the distance. Murmuring silver streams and cascading torrents pour down the mountain slopes; glaciers and snowfields creep over the precipices of Folgefonna.

Seen in spring, the innumerable orchards along the steep sides and near the sheltered creeks are a cloud of blossom; in the autumn, the trees bend under the weight of the red and golden fruit (pears, apples and cherries). The blue fjord below and the white snow above form a startling colour contrast. The many waterfalls — *Vøringsfoss, Tyssestrengene, Skjeggedalsfoss* and *Låtefoss* — add splendour to the district.

There is a main road connection from Odda across the Haukeli mountains to Telemark and Eastern Norway, and through the Bratland valley to Ryfylke. A road also runs past the Vøringfoss and across the northern part of Hardangervidda to Haugastøl on the Oslo–Bergen railway, and still further east where it connects with the roads of Eastern Norway.

The people of Hardanger have a high standard of home-craft (wood-carving, weaving and embroidery).

131

The Fishmarket in Bergen with the Hanseatic Wharf.

Bergen and Hordaland.

Bergen, Norway's second city was founded in 1070 A. D., and in spite of repeated fires and other disasters during the centuries, the city is still rich in relics of its ancient culture and traditions that give it a character of its own among the cities and towns of Norway.

Owing to its favourable location, Bergen soon became one of the most important towns along the coast, and already in the Middle Ages it was a thriving commercial centre frequented by merchants from countries all round the North Sea. The inhabitants of the town came into closer contact with the surrounding world than did the rest of the country, and this has given them a cosmopolitan quality, a broadmindedness and a freedom from prejudice which, however, in no way make them less Norwegian than the rest. Moreover, one finds in Bergen a strong and sincere affection for the native town, and a feeling for urban tradition that is but rarely found elsewhere in Norway.

And who can escape being captivated by this charming city, beautifully situated in matchless surroundings of imposing mountains and a smiling ocean opening a view to the world? Standing on top of the "Fløyen" mountain on a bright summer day, with the delightful panorama of

the roofs and spires of the city and the glittering blue of the fjord, the busy life in the harbour and on the broad, open streets in the centre of the city, one will agree that few cities in the world are able to offer a more enchanting spectacle.

This impression is not changed by a walk through the city. Open, modern streets alternate with quaint old alleys, and representative buildings with idyllic little houses of a bygone age. One is aware of being in a city with an atmosphere of its own, witty and unsentimental.

Bergen to-day has nearly 110,000 inhabitants, including the suburbs nearly 140,000. Although Bergen is far from being a "museum town" devoting all its time and efforts to the preservation of memories of former greatness, it is natural to mention first some of the old buildings, such as the old town hall from 1558, one of the few houses in the centre of the town that escaped unharmed in the great fire of 1916. The lovely old churches, of which the city is justly proud, are also well preserved: *Domkirken* (The Cathedral), originally a Franciscan church from the 13th Century; *Korskirken* and *Mariakirken* (The German Church) from the 12th Century, and *Nykirken*, which was severely damaged by an explosion during the last war.

The same explosion also caused great damage to the

Rosenkrantz Tower was built in the 16th Century to maintain the power of the Crown against the Hanseatic merchants.

most interesting block of ancient structures in the city: The old fortress *Bergenhus* with the tower *Rosenkrantz Tårn* and *Håkonshallen*, a royal hall from the Middle Ages which had been decorated by the painter Gerhard Munthe.

On the way out to the fortress one passes *"Bryggen"* (The Wharf), which has preserved some of its characteristic old wooden structures that were typical of medieval commercial towns. One of the buildings now contains *The Hanseatic Museum*, which is fitted with furniture and equipment from the days when German merchants still dominated the commerce of the town.

In the suburb of Sandviken a local museum has recently been created. It comprises some 60 houses, *"Old Bergen"*, forming a little town from the 18th and 19th Centuries which gives an intimate and lively picture of what the poet has called "the droll city behind the vapoury sky".

Bergen is the seat of a number of educational and research institutions, and in 1948 the city got its *University*, to which several institutes are affiliated, among them the well-known *Geophysical Institute*. In keeping with the tradions of the city, the *State College of Commerce and Economics* was also placed in Bergen. The theatre, *Den Nasjonale Scene*, which was founded in 1850, plays

an important part in the cultural life. *The Bergen Museum* contains rich collections of natural and cultural history. Among the many other collections special mention must be made of the *Rasmus Meyer Collections* of Modern Norwegian Art.

The economic life is still dominated by commerce and shipping, but industry is growing steadily, and especially in the surrounding districts there is a number of important factories (canning, textiles, margarine, flour mills and shipyards).

In the immediate vicinity of the city there are many charming spots that lovers of nature will delight in visiting. A funicular railway takes one up to the mountain *"Fløyfjellet"*, 960 feet above the city, where there is a magnificent view and a good restaurant. From Fløyen there are many refreshing walks to be made through the mountain regions. By the lovely lake Nordåsvann lies *"Trollhaugen"* the home of *Edvard Grieg*, with objects of great interest to friends of music, and *"Gamlehaugen"*, the home of the illustrious statesman *Chr. Michelsen*, which has been made into a royal residence where the King stays when visiting Bergen. In the same vicinity we have the famous *Fantofts stave-church*.

Bergen is the point of departure for trips to the magnificent fjords of Western Norway, making it a great

133

In the centre of Bergen lies a little lake surrounded by parks and public buildings.

tourist centre. The beautiful trip across the mountains to Oslo by the Bergen—Oslo railway is an outstanding attraction. There are aeroplane connections with America, England and the Continent, and a great number of passenger ships both from foreign and domestic ports call at Bergen. A trip through Norway may well be started in Bergen, but the traveller will not regret spending some of his time in getting to know this city with its lovely parks and interesting museums, its excellent hotels and well-equipped stores.

The coastal territory adjacent to *Bergen* is called *Hordaland*. It has densely populated large and small islands, narrow valleys, green plains and small blue lakes lying amid rugged, grey mountains. The districts to the north of Bergen are termed *Nordhordland*, the vicinity of Bergen itself, *Midthordland*, and that bordering on the outer Hardangerfjord is called *Sunnhordland*. These parts have nothing particularly imposing or grand to offer but the scenery varies greatly. Smiling, fruitful acres lie between steep, rocky crags; there are forested valleys and lakes, sheltered bays with the fishermen's huts, and the vegetation is as luxuriant as the climate is mild and humid.

About 6 miles south of Bergen is *Lyse kloster*, the ruins of a Cistercian monastery. Further south at *Os*, the landscape is open, and there is a charming view of the Hardanger mountains and the Folgefonn glacier.

Sogn.

Sognefjorden is the longest and deepest fjord in Norway. It runs west to east, penetrating about 110 miles into the country, and in some places reaching a depth of more than 3,500 feet. It branches off in a number of directions, in a landscape which is greatly diversified with smiling, idyllic scenery alternating with views having an almost gloomy, dismal character: Bluish-black mountains that nearly take your breath away.

There is nothing very unusual about the landscape in the outer part of the fjord. But then — about half-way in — the main branch of the fjord turns north and opens upon the most magnificent views. In the north lies *Balestrand* (Balholm) with villas and hotels surrounded by delightful fruit orchards, and in the background a mighty mountain rises steeply 4,800 feet into the air.

At Balestrand, a narrow, lovely fjord cuts northwards through a rugged landscape adorned with great glaciers and enormous snowfields.

A little farther in the main fjord, the town of *Leikanger* is situated in a district which is in effect a virtual fruit orchard. To the south is *Vik* with an old, interesting church. The Saga of Fridtjof and Ingeborg is identified with this region.

Still farther in, the Sognefjord again cuts north and reaches lovely, fertile *Sogndal*.

A branch of the fjord — *Aurlandsfjorden* — runs southwards to *Flåm*, whence a road and railway lead up through the steep valley of *Flåmsdalen* to Myrdal Station on the Bergen—Oslo railway. (See also page 99.) Branching off from the Aurlandsfjord, a very narrow fjord proceeds in a southwesterly direction towards *Gudvangen*, which is linked to Stalheim and Voss by a road running up through the valley.

Farthest in, the main fjord branches off in three directions. One of the branches leads in to *Lærdalsøyra*, a fjord-side township at the mouth of the river Lærdals-

134

View of Fjærland, Sogn.

elven, which is famous for its excellent salmon fishing. From Lærdalsøyra a road leads across the mountain of Filefjell and down into the valleys of Valdres, Hemsedal and Hallingdal. Halfway up the valley is the *Borgund* stave-church, which dates back to the 12th Century. This is one of the most beautiful and best preserved churches of its kind in Norway (see illustr. P. 14.)

From the head of the next fjord, *Årdalsfjorden*, a road runs along the lake Årdalsvatnet, which is green in color from the glacier water, to the factory town of Øvre Årdal. On all sides are seen the overwhelming mountains of western Jotunheimen. In a narrow valley which cuts inland in a northeasterly direction we have the highest waterfall in Norway, *Vettisfossen*, with an almost perpendicular drop of 780 feet. A steep, serpentine road runs eastwards to the mountain lake of Tyin.

The third fjord, *Lusterfjorden*, continues far north to *Skjolden*, passing fertile and charming little bights lying under precipitous mountain crags. On the western side of the fjord lies the lovely old *Urnes* stave-church (see illustration P. 13).

One of the most important roads in the district connects Leikanger—Sogndal—Skjolden. A branch of this road passes through the narrow, sparsely populated valley of Jostedal up to where the glacier Jostedalsbreen

sends its magnificent arms down along the mountainsides. From Skjolden a road runs eastwards, ascending steeply up to *Turtagrø* at the foot of the mountains Skagastølstindene (7,200 feet high). (See also page 60.) In summer the road is open across the mountain plateau to Lom on the other side of the watershed. Busses operate on all major roads.

Sunnfjord.

Sunnfjord lies between Sogn in the south and Nordfjord in the north. The whole district is scarred by long valleys and fjords which go from east to west. To the east and south-east the mountains tower, crowned by dazzling white snow: the *Jostedal glacier*. The islands which hug the coast are comparatively small and bare. On one of these islands the small commercial and industrial centre of *Florø* (pop. 1,500) is to be found. On the island *Kinn* an interesting stone church, dating back to about 1050 A. D., can be seen. To the north-east of Florø is the electric power station *Svelgen*, which gains its power from the melting ice and snow of the Ålfot glacier (4,800 ft.). This beautiful glacier branches towards *Nordfjord* in the north, and to the west of the glacier fantastically shaped mountains climb towards the sky.

The Nigard glacier, a branch of Jostedalsbreen.

Lake Loenvatn.

From *Vadheim* by the *Sognefjord* a main road leads to *Førde*, a fertile agricultural district in the apex of the Førdefjord. The road continues eastwards through *Jølster*, a valley known for its impressive beauty. The Jølster lake lies like a green mirror reflecting every imaginable shade of green from the surrounding meadows, forest and hillside. The heavy, solid mountains loom high above this charming landscape, reaching a height of 5,000 feet, with their peaks covered by flake-white snow. Nikolai Astrup, a great artist, has made this region famous through his paintings.

From Jølster the road leads on to Nordfjord.

Nordfjord.

Nordfjord includes all the districts which lie along the fjord of that name. The 60 mile-long Nordfjord is the second longest in West Norway, and the countryside around the inner parts of the fjord ranks high among the beautiful parts of Norway. On an island at the mouth of the fjord towers the rocky *Hornelen* (2,700 ft.), the ancient Smalsahorn, which according to the sagas was long considered insurmountable, but was ultimately climbed by King Olav Trygvason, nearly 1,000 years ago. On another island lies *Måløy*, a fishing and industrial centre which was raided by the British during the German Occupation. Further along the fjord, an arm branches off and leads to *Nordfjordeid*, a densely populated village, from where a road runs eastwards along the extremely beautiful lake Hornindalsvatn to the well-known tourist centres *Hellesylt* and *Øye* in Sunnmøre, and *Loen, Olden* and *Stryn* at the end of Nordfjord. Here the scenery attains its most imposing beauty, and assumes proportions of supreme grandeur, particularly in the vicinity of the small, imprisoned lakes Oldenvatnet and Loenvatnet. Caught between precipitous mountain walls rising to a height of 6,000 ft. are the green, burnished lakes, and, cascading into them, are silvery rills and brooks from the snow-covered peaks.

Farthest inland the dazzling glaciers creep to the very edge of the valley head: *Briksdalsbreen, Krunsbreen, Kjenndalsbreen* etc.

Wm. Cecil Slingsby, the English mountaineer, writes: "... a scene of marvellous beauty was presented to us as we rowed down the Olden Vand on a summer night in soft and silvery moonlight. The wavy snow-fields and glistening ice, intensely pure by contrast with the dark shadows under the steep mountains were reflected upon the glassy surface of the lake. *St. Cecilia Krone*

137

The Nordfjord horse is a sturdy and reliable working comrade.

(The Crown of St. Cecily) towered above us, and glittering in the moonlight, her tiny glacier looked like a necklace of pearls hanging gracefully over her shoulders. The deathlike stillness, alone broken by the splash of oars, seemed hardly of this world. Each one felt it to be a time for thinking, and not for talking, and each of us will treasure in our memories this scene as being one of the most impressive in the storehouse of nature."

The same may be said of Loenvatnet. In 1936 a great catastrophe occured, when huge pieces of the mountainside fell into the sea and caused a destructive wave, burying farms and people.

From Stryn the main road runs eastwards along the excellent salmon river Strynselva, and continues along the south slope of the delightful lake Strynsvatn, lying in a fertile forest district which supports many farms, and with mountains dominating on every side. Proceeding up the Hjelle valley, rising steeply in many loops, the road reaches the Videseter tourist station, where one has a unique view of the green lakes, blue fjords, the fields, mountain moors and snow tracts of Nordfjord. Continuing and still climbing, the road crosses the plateau summit at Grotli, and falls away to the south-east through Skjåk, Lom and Vågå to Otta on the Dovre railway line.

Nordfjord is famed for its horse-breeding, the horse being called "Nordfjording" or merely "Fjording".

Sunnmøre.

Long fjords, twisting and turning to the south and east, divide the country into a number of large peninsulas. In the east, the country rises steeply to form enormous mountain ranges with summits of up to 6,000 feet. Beyond these are the eternally snow-clad regions (across which one can drive to the Gudbrandsdal).

The scenery varies greatly. Smiling, fertile districts like *Ørsta* and *Volda*, framed by delicate pinnacles and peaks, contrast with wild fjord and mountain regions like *Hjørundfjord*, *Norangsdal*, *Sunnylven* and *Geiranger*.

The mountains of Sunnmøre are more like the Swiss Alps than the mountains in Nordfjord and Sogn, their profiles being sharper and more varied in shape. The fantastically shaped mountains of Norangsdal are typical in this respect. In the narrow Geirangerfjord, the famous waterfalls of the "Bridal Veil" and the "Seven Sisters", so called because of its seven arms, fall straight into the fjord from great heights. At the upper end of *Tafjord* is the magnificent spectacle of the Muldal fall.

From Meråk in the bottom of the Geirangerfjord climbs a steep road with hair-pin bends, which leads to *Grotli* where it joins the road from Stryn. One can reach the summit of *Dalsnibba* (5,100 ft.) by car. From this mountain top one has a wonderful view of the surround-

The famous panorama of Molde towards the Vestnes range.

ing mountain region. One can drive from *Valldal* in Tafjord to *Åndalsnes* in Romsdal. This is the *Trollstegvei*, known as one of the most remarkable roads in Norway, passing through scenery of incomparable beauty.

Lying off the mainland towards the sea in the west are a number of densely populated islands. Situated on a peninsula is *Ålesund* (pop. 18,000), the principal town of the district. This is a busy fishing port, which also is the home base for the important seal catching in Arctic waters. Most of the town was left in ashes after the large fire of 1904, and in April 1940 and later during the war the town was bombed.

Romsdal.

Romsdal includes the country round the Romsdalsfjord and its branches as well as the two valleys *Eikesdal* and *Romsdal (Rauma)* proper, continuing in the direction of the fjord. The outer fjord is broad and its main course is from west to east. On the north shore lies *Molde*, known for its fertile and gentle surroundings, its old trees and its wealth of flowers. From Molde one has a beautiful view of the Romsdal mountains. The national poet Bjørnstjerne Bjørnson attended school at Molde, and it was here that Henrik Ibsen found the motiv for

"The Lady from the Sea". During recent years the manufacturing industry has become of great importance, and apart from this, export of fish and fish products is the main industry in the town. Molde, which received its township in 1742, was damaged by a great fire in 1916, and was again damaged by German bombs in 1940.

Proceeding inland, the upper part of the fjord becomes more and more narrow, with ever steeper and more imposing banks; at the mouth of the Rauma, on the west bank of the river, is the old trading centre *Veblungsnes*, and on the east side lies the railway terminus *Åndalsnes*, a new town situated in idyllic surroundings. From Åndalsnes the road leads to Trollstegveien and Valldal. The valley proper commences at Veblungsnes, and through the valley runs a main road and the Rauma railway line which, at first with a slight gradient and later more steeply, climbs the valley through tunnels and loops, and proceeds towards the *Dovre* mountains.

The mountain regions of Romsdal present a panorama of exceptional grandeur. Here, concentrated in a comparatively small area, are several of Norway's highest and most impressive mountains: Romsdalshorn, Venjetindene, Trolltindene, etc., all more than 5,000 feet high.

The main branch of Romsdalsfjord, *Langfjord*, first takes an easterly direction, then turns south into the

139

Romsdalshorn, the most imposing peak
of the Romsdal Mountains.

valley of Eikesdal. Squeezed down between mighty mountain walls which attain a height of 5,500 feet, is the beautiful lake *Eikesdal*. It was here, while staying on the old farm, Utigard, that Bjørnson, in the summer of 1858, wrote "Arne", one of his first peasant novels, in which he described the scenery of Romsdal thus:

«There was a deep ravine between two of the mountains; through it a full-flowing stream rushed heavily down over boulder and crag. High was the bank on each hand, and rocky, so that one side stood barren and naked; but close to the stream and so near it that in spring and autumn it shook its spray upon them, were green patches of forest-growth, looking up and around, and finding room to throw out their arms neither here nor there . . . 'What if we were to clothe the ravine-side,' said the juniper —."

Nordmøre.

Facing north towards the coastal waters named *Griphavet* and *Hustadvika*, is the county of *Nordmøre*. A number of large islands forms its outskirts; further inland are the long, curving fjords, with forest-clad banks and snug creeks giving shelter to clusters of houses; while farthest inland come the narrow valleys, winding a path between rocky mountain walls up to the regions of *Trollheimen* and *Dovre*.

On three small, bare islands towards Griphavet is the only town of the district, *Kristiansund* (pop. 13,000). Its main industry is the production and export of split cod; in sumer the major part of the population is busy with the fish, which is spread out to dry on every naked cliff and headland. The town was practically destroyed by German bombing in April—May 1940, but is now rapidly being rebuilt.

The fjords branch out in fan-shape into the country from Kristiansund, the long *Trollfjord* in a south-easterly direction towards *Sunndalsøyra*, *Halsafjord* slightly more eastward and *Vinjefjord* to the east. Towards the north-east and facing the approach to Trondheimsfjord is the open sea. There is a beautiful stave-church at *Gjemnes* in the outer fjord; and on the east bank of the fjord is *Tingvoll*, a delightful spot in a sheltered bay with rich vegetation, where there is a stone church built about 1200 A. D. Further inland, Sunndalsfjord is flanked by wonderful scenery. On each side of the fjord are steep, forested banks with lonely farms here and there, and at Sunndalsøyra, at the end of the fjord, the mountains climb to an altitude of 5,500 ft. A road runs through the valley *Sunndal*, well-known for its beauty, and continues through the wild and narrow valley *Drivdal* to *Opdal*, on the Dovre railway line.

From the friendly parish of *Stangvik* at Halsafjord another main road proceeds eastward and soon reaches the broad, well-cultivated valleys of *Surnadal* and *Rindal*, through which one can reach *Sør-Trøndelag*, the broad districts to the south of Trondheimsfjord.

Between Sunndal in the south and Rindal in the north lies the scarred, wild mountain district of *Trollheimen* (the Home of the Trolls, or Giants). Deep, narrow val-

Glimpse of the beautiful Inderdal in Nordmøre.

leys slash through the mountain region in all directions, and the mountains rise straight up to a height of 5,000 ft.

The beauty of Nordmøre forms a natural transition from that of Trøndelag. The population of Nordmøre is strongly intermixed with the people of Trøndelag, and the mood and language of the former have also assumed a Trøndelag-like tone and colouring. Even the style of house construction found further up the valleys becomes that of Trøndelag. We have to admit, therefore, that in reality we are no longer in West-Norway proper. However, when travelling in West-Norway, it would be natural to include a trip to the beauty of Nordmøre before turning south or east, and therefore the county has been included here.

141

A typical «seter» — a summer dairy farm in the mountains.

THE MOUNTAIN DISTRICTS
of Southern Norway.

MORE THAN HALF of Norway lies above the tree limit. In southern Norway the forests rarely climb beyond 2,500—2,700 feet, while in the North the tree limit is considerably lower. Mountains of Alpine character with sharp peaks and torn sides are only to be found in certain parts of the western and northern coastal regions. The major part of the Norwegian mountains take the form of a vast *highland plateau* with an average height of 3,000 feet, from which again massive mountains rise. This highland plateau stretches from south to north through the whole of southern Norway, from the moors of Sørlandet in the south to Trøndelag in the north. At *Hardangervidda* it broadens out to become a typical highland plateau, and further north it continues into Norway's mightiest mountain range, *Jotunheimen*. Still further north and east it forms the broad districts of *Dovre*, and the picturesque *Rondane* chain.

Before giving a more detailed account of these mountain regions, we will describe the typical highland scene in Norway. After leaving the valley, the highland unfolds itself; a gently undulating plateau with innumerable lakes and tarns, shining like mirrors in the clear mountain air. This is not an empty world, even though above the tree limit. On the contrary, the Norwegian mountain districts are rich in fresh grass, heather, low bushes and colourful flowers. Farms in the valley send their cattle up to the highlands in summer; here are the richest pastures in Norway, and here are the summer-farms, or *seters*, — low, idyllic houses with grass roofs. This is a world of its own, a peaceful world with but few traces of civilisation, where it is possible to walk for days along the paths and tracks through unspoiled nature. It is an easy climb to reach the mountains which rise from the plateau. This is a hikers' paradise in every sense of the word. The Norwegian Touring Club (Den Norske Turistforening) and local associations have built a lot of huts in these regions, with an easy day's walk between them, where the hiker can procure a healthy, simple meal and a good night's rest. These huts are open from the end of June until sometime in September, and also in the Easter holiday.

Hardangervidda.

Hardangervidda, or simply "Vidda" (an open highland) as it is popularly termed, is the vast district comprising the highest moorlands in Norway. As usually understood, "Vidda" is the region lying south of *Hallingskarvet*, east of *Sørfjord* and *Eidfjord* in Hardanger, west of the *Numedal* and *Hallingdal* valleys, and north of the *Haukeli* mountains.

In the centre of the plateau are the lakes, richly stocked with fish, and numerous waters and streams which form the source of the mighty water-courses of Hallingdalselv

142

Horses grazing on the open highland plateaus.

and Numedalslågen, running east, and Bjoreia and Veig running west. In recent years many tourist huts have been built on Hardangervidda. Wild reindeer still live on the southern moors, but the herds are greatly diminished.

Hardangervidda proper is bordered to the north-east by the clear-cut rocky wall of *Hallingskarvet* (5,700 ft.), and to the north-west by the mighty snow-covered dome of the *Hardangerjøkel* — a glacier which also reaches a height of 5,700 ft. Towards the east, "Vidda" falls gently to the valleys, but in the west it ends abruptly in precipices, falling straight down to the fjords of Hardanger.

From ancient times the much-used paths of traffic between Hardanger and the upper valleys of East-Norway have crossed Hardangervidda, and centuries-old, hard-trodden paths are still clearly marked.

The charm and attraction of Hardangervidda lies in the wide, open spaces, the large lakes, the many mountains and, in the north-west, the falls and glaciers. To the south is the isolated, hat-like summit, *Hårteigen* (5,067 ft.), rising like a lighthouse from the moors and a landmark to be seen from all sides. To the north gleams the icy dome of the Hardangerjøkel with its crevassed, black peaks. In the west, the *Vøringsfoss waterfall* (489 ft.) falls perpendicularly down into the wild Måbø valley, and the beautiful waters of *Valursfoss* drop more than 300 feet into Hjalmodal.

The motoring road coming from the east (Hallingdal and Numedal) crosses Hardangervidda on its way west to Hardanger. Having passed *Haugastøl* on the Oslo—Bergen railway line, there is much of beauty and wonder to be seen. Proceeding south of the Hardangerjøkel gla-

cier, the road passes Vøringsfoss and, curving gracefully, winds its way down the steep, rocky wall of the Måbø valley to Eidfjord in Hardanger.

Jotunheimen.

Jotunheimen, which in Norwegian mythology was the home of the giants and trolls, is the mountain region lying in the centre of southern Norway. It is a district of mighty mountains, glaciers, lakes and valleys, situated between the upper valleys of Gudbrandsdal in the east and north, Valdres in the south and Inner Sogn in the west. With its peaks of more than 7,000 feet, this mountain group is the highest not only in Norway but in the whole of Northern Europe as well. The district is intersected by narrow, wild ravine-like valleys.

Jotunheimen is divided by Utladal into two parts. In East Jotunheimen are the highest peaks of the entire region, *Galdhøpiggen* (7,407 ft.) and *Glitretind* (7,353 ft.); while in West Jotunheimen is the group of crevassed peaks known as *Skagastølstindene* (Horungene), of which the highest is Store Skagastølstind (Storen) (7,212 ft.). In the southern part of Jotunheimen are the large, delightful lakes *Gjende*, *Bygdin* and *Tyin*. Lake *Gjende* in particular is entrancingly beautiful with its green-tinted glacier water, flanked by *Besseggen*, *Bessbø*, *Knutholstind* and other peaks of more than 6,900 feet. Access to the lakes is now easy as good roads lead to all three from Gudbrandsdal and Valdres. There are good hotels and tourist hostels in the vicinity.

Many snowfields light up the chain of dark mountains, the largest glaciers being *Fanaråken* and *Smør-*

143

The mountain regions are rich in fresh grass, heather and colourful flowers.

stabbreen in West Jotunheimen. To the north of Fanaråken runs a narrow road from Sogn to Gudbrandsdal, crossing the Sogn mountain group at 4,200 feet. The view is magnificent, and there are plans being made for the construction of a modern road, capable of taking motor traffic, approximately following the ancient track. On the summit of Fanaråken, at a height of 6,225 feet above the sea level, is a combined meteorological station and tourist hut. Tourist huts are also to be found in the valleys and near the various lakes. A small hut for resting after the ascent lies on the top of Galdhøpiggen. There is a narrow motoring road from Bøverdal to Juvasshytta, a hostel some 2,000 feet below the summit of Galdhøpiggen.

Jotunheimen is much visited by tourists on foot during the summer, and by skiers at Easter-time. Near the mouth of lake *Gjende* the river is particularly full of trout. There are still a few wild reindeer in the district, but their number is rapidly decreasing. The tame reindeer, however, are numerous, and live happily here.

Dovre.

Dovre, or Dovrefjell, is the name given to the mighty stretch of mountainous country dividing the *nordenfjellske* ("north-of-the-mountains"), Trøndelag and Nordmøre, from the *søndenfjellske* ("south-of-the-mountains"), Østlandet. Broad, solid mountains with peaks attaining more than 6,000 feet in height rise from the highland pastures at 3,000 feet above sea level. To the north is *Snøhetta* (6,855 ft.), the eastern outpost of this gigantic mountain group which extends towards Sunndal in Nordmøre in the north and in the south towards Dombås in Gudbrandsdal.

Across the Dovre mountains ran the ancient road which linked Østlandet with Trøndelag. Today, roughly following the same track and connecting these two parts of the country, runs the main road and the Dovre railway line with its stations of *Fokstua, Hjerkinn, Kongsvoll* and *Drivstua* on the same sites as the old saddling stations and inns.

Lake Gjende in the heart of Jotunheimen.

Snøhetta rises above the wide expanse of the Dovre plateau.

146

The summits of Rondane.

At *Fokstua* is Fokstumyra, a lengthy stretch of marshy country now preserved by law as a bird sanctuary. The Dovre region is also known for its rich and varied flora, and steps have been taken to preserve the rare plants.

In the popular mind, the Dovre mountains stand for all that is permanent and impregnable in Norway—the rallying point of the country. "Enig og tro til Dovre faller" (united we stand till the Dovre mountains fall)— goes the saying which symbolizes the Norwegian feeling of unity.

Milking the goats on the seter.

Rondane.

An isolated rocky massif, *Rondane* lies at the south-east corner of Dovre, between Gudbrandsdal and Østerdal. A chain of gracefully formed peaks attain heights of more than 6,000 feet, Rondeslottet, Høgronden and Storronden being the highest.

Rondane is one of the most charming of the Norwegian mountain regions — a region which lures many Norwegians and foreigners to it every year, summer and winter. Paths have been clearly marked here as in the other mountain districts, and the tourist clubs have built huts at suitable intervals all through the chain.

147

Old warehouses on the river Nidelv in Trondheim.

TRØNDELAG

TRØNDELAG is the extensive agricultural and forest country lying around the long *Trondheimsfjord*, including the many broad valleys leading inland in every direction. In their lower districts the valleys are wide and flat with well-kept farms and large buildings. Further inland, however, they usually become narrow with forest-clad slopes and scattered population. Rich salmon rivers flow through these valleys, and here and there are magnificent waterfalls like *Fiskemfossen* (105 feet) in the Namsen river, and Upper and Lower *Leirfossen* (105 and 84 feet) on the river *Nid*, just south of Trondheim.

Where the Nid flows out into the Trondheimsfjord, King Olav Trygvason founded, in 998 A. D., the market town which in the course of the years has been called Nidaros, Trondhjem and *Trondheim*. For centuries the intellectual centre of Norway, and the favourite residence of the Kings, it remained the chief ecclesiastical city of the kingdom until the Reformation.

The market-place of Trondheim is adorned by a statue of Olav Trygvason, the founder of the city.

The Choir of the Trondheim Cathedral.

Trondheim is a fine city with open, broad thoroughfares. In one of the main streets, Munkegaten, is Stiftsgården. Now used as a residence for the King when staying in the city, it is a beautiful wooden building of fine proportions. (See illustr. P. 26.) At the end of Munkegaten is the great Cathedral which was completed about 1320 A. D. It was then, without comparison, the most beautiful and splendid cathedral in the Northern countries. Its length is about 300 feet. After 1500, however, it soon fell into disrepair, suffering damage from fires on several occasions. Since 1869 extensive restoration work has been going on, and the exterior is not yet completed. Norwegian Kings are crowned in the

Cathedral. The old Archbishop's Palace near by is now a museum.

Among the numerous schools of the city is the State University College of Technology of Norway.

Trondheim is the heart of a large and rich district, Sør-Trøndelag. An excellent harbour has encouraged trade, and mines and industrial undertakings have increased the commercial importance of the city. It is the third largest town in Norway (pop. 57,000). The environs are pleasant and the scenery is varied; the historical associations are many.

Immediately to the east of the town is *Lade Kongs-gård*, a royal estate where the Earls of Lade had their

149

View of Meråker in North Trøndelag, bordering on Sweden.

seat. A stone church from the 12th Century still remains, and on the property is today a Teachers' College. On the outer Trondheimsfjord is another royal mansion, *Aust-rått*. Here, in the 16th Century, resided "Lady Inger" —immortalised by Henrik Ibsen's drama. Its beautiful main building is maintained by the State. Just outside Trondheim, on a small island, lies *Munkholmen*. First built as a monastery, it was later transformed into a fortress.

The country along the Inner Trondheimsfjord *(Inn-herad)* with the towns of *Levanger* and *Steinkjer*, is open and broad. The latter town was bombed and burnt during the war, but is now rebuilt. The farms in this districts are well managed, and the houses and churches are large, situated in rich, undulating terrain—strongly reminiscent of the vicinity of Lake Mjøsa. Further north is a third town, *Namsos*, on the inner Namsenfjord. It is the centre of the rich agricultural and forest district of the Namdal valley, which goes in a north-

east direction towards the county of Nordland. The main road and railways to Nordland run through this valley. The highway from Trøndelag to Sweden passes through *Verdal* on its way eastward. Here is the venerable church of *Stiklestad*, and the monument marking the spot where King Olav the Saint fell in 1030 A.D. On the whole, Trøndelag is rich in traditions from the Middle Ages. A railway line to Sweden runs further south via *Stjørdal*.

Manor house of a Trøndelag farm.

The Midnight Sun.

NORD-NORGE
(Northern Norway.)

THAT PART of the country which lies to the north of Trøndelag is commonly called Northern Norway. This is shaped as an enormously long narrow neck, leading in a north-easterly direction, and terminating on the 71st latitude. The entire length of Norway from Cape Lindesnes in the south to North Cape is approximately 1,060 miles. Of this length, over half belongs to Northern Norway. Towards the west and north there is a continuous coast-line consisting of innumerable islands and fjords. Except in the very north, Finnmark, the mountains reach great heights, and the landscape can be compared to that of Western Norway. More than 4/5 of Northern Norway lies within the Arctic Circle. This means that practically every citizen in this vast part of the country is familiar with the sight of the midnight sun, with days and nights when the sun never leaves the sky. As one goes further north, the number of these daylit nights increase. Conversely, they have an equal number of days in winter when the sun never rises above the horizon. Because of the Gulf Stream, which closely follows the coast-line, these northern districts have a mild winter, comparable to that of Hungary.

The tourists found their way to Northern Norway a long time ago. To travel by steamer along this varying and picturesque coast in summer is truly an adventure. The midnight sun gives an eerie light to these fjords, mountains and glaciers, which is not seen further down the coast. Until fairly recently, there was no railway and few roads in this part of the country, and the traveller was completely dependent on boats. The inner regions, however, have rich agricultural and forest districts, and it is now possible to travel by car from the extreme south to the farthest north. As yet, there are not enough hotels, but the traveller who does not demand too much will never regret a journey to these northern regions. The railway is only open as far as just north of Saltfjell, but it will not be long before Bodø can be reached by rail.

The roads are, naturally, often closed in winter— due to heavy snowfall.

The population in Northern Norway is very sparse, especially on the *Finnmark plateau*. They have mostly settled in groups round the best natural harbours along the coast. The chief occupation is fishing, but agriculture, various industries and mining are increasing.

Svartisen—The "Black Ice" Glacier.

Helgeland.

Helgeland—its name signifying ancient worship of *Aurora borealis*—is an elongated district which lies between the Swedish border in the east and the Atlantic Ocean in the west. Along the coast there are lengthy fjords, narrow and curved, and inland there are steep valleys with mighty waterfalls and large forests. Just outside the coast there are myriads of islands, and further out the ocean breaks on the skerries and sunken rocks where shoals of fish gather.

The mountains tower high, fascinating in their varying shapes and colours; and bluish-green glaciers fill the ravines of *Okstindene* and *Svartisen* (about 5,700 and 4,800 feet respectively). Well known attractions are: "*Torghatten*", an island with a quadrangular hole through the hat-shaped rock; the seven peaks named the "*Seven Sisters*"; "*Hestmannen*" island (the Horseman), a silhouette of folklore fame; and the *Rødøy* "lion" with its characteristic profile in red rock. Far out in the ocean are the islands of *Træna* and *Lovunden*, with cliffs where millions of birds breed in the steep ravines.

The walls of the *Okstind* range rise with glaciers and peaks behind the mighty basin of lake *Røsvatnet*, and the waterfalls of *Røsåen* are among the most imposing in Norway. Here are the well cultivated parishes

of *Vefsn*, *Korgen* and *Rana*, well populated and with an abundant vegetation climbing far up towards the surrounding graceful, snowcapped mountains. Well known are the fantastically shaped limestone grottos at Grønlia in *Rana*, carved by snow, ice and water. The grottos contain waterfalls and pools, strangely curved passages, galleries and colonnades, all in a rich phantasmagoria of crystals. At Mo in Rana there are large iron-works under construction, sponsored by the State.

One of the most beautiful sights of Helgeland is the small island of *Grønnøy*, just within the Arctic Circle. The island is hidden in a sheltered bay, and has luxuriant green pastures, flower meadows and old fir forests, encircled by towering bluish-black peaks, and with the mighty glacier *Svartisen* in the distance. In mid-summer, the fruit and flower gardens are close neighbours of the eternal snow, right on the Arctic Circle! The temperate and humid climate created by the warm, life-giving Gulf Stream along the coast and through the deep fjords of Helgeland produces a vegetation undreamt of in other countries on a similar latitude, such as Alaska and northern Siberia.

On the islands and by the coast the population is settled in groups, while in the valleys the farms are more scattered. The most important means of livelihood are the fisheries and, to an increasing degree, agriculture. Among the metals found in the mountains, especially

*The mighty hole
through the rock
on Torghatten Island.*

along the inner *Ranfjord* and in the *Dunderland* valley, are iron, copper, lead and zinc. Helgeland possesses great sources of water-power, but little has yet been harnessed. The most important power-stations are in Glomfjord.

It is an unforgettable experience to travel along this coast, whether on a beautiful summer night, with the bright midnight sun, or on an evening in winter with the flaming aurora borealis flickering over the sky.

It is an even greater adventure to leave the beaten track and visit the outlying islands. With the shriek and chatter of eiderdown birds and sea-gulls in the air, the boats wind their way on the narrow, twisting sounds, with groups of well-kept dwellings along the bays and creeks. By the fjords and in the valleys one finds unexpectedly broad, well-tilled fields, large farms, good roads, mighty salmon rivers and sparkling lakes which abound with trout.

The Helgelander has a happy temperament—an excellent reserve to possess when the winter storms rage and gloom settles down on the country during the long, dark period of the year.

Bodø with the Salten Mountains in the background.

Salten and Ofoten.

The mountainous region which comprises the northern part of the county of Nordland is known as *Salten*. Lying entirely within the Arctic Circle between latitude 67 and 68, it is separated from the islands of Lofoten by the broad, open waters of *Vestfjorden*. Some of the long, twisted fjords penetrate far inland, a distance of some 20 to 45 miles, between steep banks with little population. From the head of the fjords, steep mountain passes (about 7 miles long) lead eastward into Sweden.

In the vicinity of *Bodø* and Saltfjord, the landscape is similar in character to that of Helgeland, but in the north it changes character entirely. Most of the mountains have polished, bluish-grey slopes, which rise steeply. They all attain between 3,000 and 4,500 feet in height, and often assume a most fantastic formation. There are several snowfields and glaciers of appreciable size, particularly along the Swedish frontier. The oldest and most important administrative town is *Bodø*, facing seawards on the northern banks of the outer *Saltfjord*. From Bodø one has a splendid view of the mountains mentioned above; and a short motoring road leads to *Løpsfjellet* in the north, where an unusually fine view of the *Lofoten* is to be seen. Lofoten, a practically continuous chain of islands, looms like a wall above the ocean.

The midnight sun is seen at Bodø from 4th June to 8th July, the sun-less period being from about 15th to 31st of December. Bodø was bombed by the Germans in 1940, and 420 of the 760 houses in the town were totally destroyed. Today, however, the town is rapidly being rebuilt, a more beautiful Bodø than ever before. From Bodø the main road leads eastward to Fauske, where it connects with the main road from Southern Norway, which continues further north. From Sjønstå a short railway line proceeds to Sulitjelma, a mining village of some importance on the Swedish border.

Slightly east of Bodø is *Saltstrømmen*, a notorious maelstrom whose fierce, swirling current can pull down large vessels into the turbulent waters. This terrific current is caused by the tidal waters passing through the narrow sounds of the inner fjord basin. Only for a few hours at the turn of the tide is it possible for vessels to pass.

From the head of the inner Saltfjord a motoring road leads through the pleasant *Saltdal* valley, through which runs the *Saltdalselv*, an excellent salmon river. Highest up in the valley lies *Junkerdal*, a valley well known for its many rare plants, now declared a national trust.

The northern parts of the district are called *Ofoten*. This includes the area of Ofotfjord (about 47 miles long) and its adjoining waters. This fjord cuts in due east from the northern extremity of *Vestfjorden*. Round the estuary, the district is broad and open. Inland, the mountains attain a height of 4,500 feet. Many of the smaller fjords leading off Ofotfjord are also of interest, particularly *Skjomen* (the Skjomfjord), at the head of which is the well-known glacier *Frostisen*.

The largest town in Nordland is *Narvik* (pop. 10,000) an export centre for iron ore from the large Swedish mines at Kiruna and Gellivare, and it is also the point of departure for the main highway, running through the county of Troms, and for the Ofotbanen railway. The town played an important part in the second world war, during the campaign in April 1940. Several large Norwegian and German naval vessels were sunk, and the town changed hands several times in the bitter fights which took place between the Allied and Norwegian troops on the one hand, and Germans on the other. In the course of this fighting the town was badly damaged, but is now rapidly being rebuilt.

The Ofotbanen railway line runs eastward to Boden on the Bothnian Gulf.

The herring fisheries in the Saltfjord are usually good. In the inner fjord areas are permanent Lapp settlements.

Lofoten and Vesterålen.

Lofoten is the name given to the long chain of islands which goes from *Skomvær* in the south-west to *Tjeldsundet* in the north-east. This chain of mountainous islands lies to the west of the broad, open *Vestfjord*. To the north-east are a number of large islands intersected by narrow ocean passages with fierce currents — like *Raftsund* and others. The mighty tidal current known as *Moskenstrømmen* — depicted on ancient maps as a large eddy, a maelstrom mercilessly pulling ships and boats into the depths — runs between the islands *Moskenesøy* and *Værøy*, where the gigantic waters of the Vestfjord ebb into the Norwegian Sea only to return into the fjord again when the tide turns.

Viewed from a distance, Lofoten seems like a wall of rock, about 70 miles long, surmounted by high, rocky peaks. The steep, pinnacled rocks, 2,000–3,000 feet high, seem to be one solid chain, but on approaching, the wall splits up into many separate islands with a number of fantastically shaped peaks. The narrow shores are green, and the azure summits are frequently cut up by reddish ravines and dazzling white drifts of snow. Around the larger islands lie many smaller, where one finds gaily painted fishing hamlets. Along the inner coast are the more important settlements, like the villages of Svolvær and Kabelvåg. In summer, when the midnight sun throws everything into strong relief, when the sounds are busy, and the bird-life provides a never-ceasing accompaniment, Lofoten is beautiful and charming. But in winter, Lofoten is much more—a place, pulsating with life, where the boats go straight out to the ocean, when everyone is busy with the fish, and the mountains are lashed by stinging snowstorms. This is when Lofoten should be seen, in the February and March season. With 20–30,000 men manning the 10,000 vessels, it certainly is a busy scene!

Through *Raftsund* the steamer passes en route to *Vesterålen* (the shore facing the Western Ocean). From Raftsund branches the narrow *Trollfjord*, well-known for its magnificent scenery. Outside Vesterålen are a

Millions of sea-birds nest on rocky islands.

155

A glimpse of Lofoten in the fishing season.

156

Målselvdal in Troms offers an unexpected picture of fertility near the Arctic circle.

number of large islands, Hadseløy, Andøy and others. The principal means of livelihood in this district is fishing. Agriculture, however, is of increasing importance, and fresh land is constantly being tilled. On Hadseløy, famed for its beauty, lie the small villages of *Melbo* and *Stokmarknes*, with considerable industrial activity.

Troms.

The county of *Troms* lies between latitude 69 and 70, thus being on a level with the north coast of Alaska. As in Helgeland and Salten, the county is split up by a number of magnificent fjords, of which the most important is *Lyngsfjord*.

The mountain formation is rather more massive than that of Nordland. The mountains being less steep, the valleys are broader, and there are large plains and broad fjords throughout the county. The mountains, moreover, do not appear to be as high as they actually are (up to 6,000 feet). Troms is also characterised by its broad, far-stretching forest valleys, reminiscent of Østerdalen. Especially rich are those in the neighbourhood of the mighty waterfalls of *Målselven* and *Barduelven*.

A net of roads serves the inner districts from Narvik in the south to Lyngsfjord in north. Inland, at latitude 69, are large pine woods and well-kept farms; here are the large waterfalls of Bardufoss (90 ft.) and Malangfoss (66 ft.) with the longest salmon-pass in the country. In the far distance tower the alpine peaks, forming a worthy frame for this beautiful district.

Along the large fjords in the north, however, it is quite different: Threatening mountains tower into clouds of snow, and on the steep, grassy slopes along the rugged coast are seen small farms, far apart. This is a region of wild grandeur. The population in the northern half of the county is considerable inter-mingled with Lapps. The people living in some of these districts have for generations had their work in the Arctic seas and icefields, hunting, fishing and trapping for seal, walrus and polar bears.

About half-way up the coast of the county is a small, green island on which lies *Tromsø*, the bishop's seat. This is a town of 11,000 inhabitants, whose chief industry is export of fish and fish products, fur and cod liver oil. Among the institutions of Tromsø are an Arctic Museum, a Geophysical Institute and an Observatory of the northern lights (Aurora borealis). The surroundings are delightful. On the islands in the west and on the mainland in the east are graceful summits which are partially covered with snow. All traffic for Finnmark, the Murman Coast and Arctic waters passes through Tromsø.

On the endless plains of Finnmark the Lapplanders still lead their traditional nomadic life as reindeer herdsmen.

The steamer route, passing inside the large islands of *Senja*, *Kvaløy* and others, leads through magnificent scenery where fertile meadows and large farms may be seen. The mountain panoramas far inland to the east and westward toward the ocean proper are of rare beauty; but it is when the midnight sun draws its multi-coloured veil over the landscape, or when the Aurora Borealis flickers across the sky, that one feels in another world, in a fairy-tale land.

Interesting monuments of mediaeval architecture are found at *Trondenes*, with its 700 years old stone church, just north of Harstad, and *Bjarkøy*, a seat of feudal chieftains during early Middle Ages.

Fishing settlements cling to the outer coast of the islands, along the small fjords and on the storm-swept promontories jutting out into the open sea. Though the environment is harsh, the sea teems with fish and birdlife is abundant.

Tromsø, the Capital of Arctic Norway.

Finnmark.

Finnmark, the northermost county of Norway, is a long stretch of country which curves eastward and south-east, facing the Arctic Ocean at about latitude 71. It is highest in the north-west and falls away towards east and south-east, finally to merge into the plains of Finland.

The coast is of naked, grey rock, unprotected and open to the storms and spray of the Arctic Sea. Here the fishing settlements are windblown, and the people are hardy, frugal folk striving stubbornly against the mighty natural forces on sea and land. But the people of Finnmark never leave their county — nowhere else will they find the 2½ months of continuous light, night and day, which so attract both the people and the migratory birds. It is because of the mild, warm summer and the rich ocean that people can live by this coast.

Thousands of tourists flock to the *North Cape* to watch the purple and gold sun curtsy into the sea and rise again, without having disappeared below the horizon. Here even the flowers take advantage of the continuous light, reaching their full bloom in an incredibly short time. On the other islands there is an abundant marine bird life. These birds breed in millions, and live happily through the summer months. But when the daylight finally dwindles, and the sun is absent for months (end of November—middle of January) life becomes hard even for semi-arctic birds.

Where the coast curves eastwards, a number of large fjords — *Altafjord, Porsangerfjord, Laksefjord* and *Tanafjord,* — cut deeply into the country southwards. Large salmon rivers run into the fjords, and along these there are clusters of farms and houses. The population is very varied, there being a large group of Lapps and Quains (Finlanders) in the county. At the head of Porsanger-fjord a group of peaks, *Gaisene,* rise to a height of about 3,000 feet, but beyond the fjord the expanses of Finnmark really commence, a far-stretching, gently undulating plain with many lakes and waterfalls, mile after mile of forest or moors southwards towards the Swedish frontier. It is on these plains that the nomadic Lapps live. In their gaily-coloured costumes, guarding their reindeer, they are to be found by the coast in summer, on the plains in winter. Their two centres, *Karasjok* and *Kautokeino,* are especially busy at Easter-time, when the annual market is on, and when they all come in to be married, or to have their children baptized. A recently constructed road now leads from Hammerfest to Kara-sjok, from where it proceeds to Finland.

In Finnmark, all towns, villages, harbour constructions and even single farms were totally destroyed by the Germans during the war. To reconstruct what has been destroyed is a work of many years, but already the whole population is back, and communications, hospitals and schools are rebuilt, as well as most farms and houses.

In East Finnmark, where the coast turns southward, is the port of *Vardø,* its ancient fortress *Vardøhus* forming the most advanced outpost to the east. The Varangerfjord here takes a turn in a westerly direction; on its southern bank is *Sør-Varanger* with its iron-mines and pine forests, the latter stretching towards the *Pasvik* valley bordering on Russia.

With its strange landscape, the eerie light, with abundant salmon rivers, plenty of game and moors full of the cloud-berry, with Lapps in gay costumes and their reindeer, Finnmark is a part of Norway which cannot be compared to anything else. Despite the mosquito — harmless but irritating — one will never regret a summer visit to this enchanting region. And in winter, with the broad

North Cape, the northermost promontory of Europe.

highland covered in a thick carpet of dazzling snow, skiing or reindeer-sleighing under the aurora borealis are sports which will thrill enthusiasts and make the beginner come back again, captivated by the fairy-tale atmosphere and strange life of Finnmark.

The fisheries represent the chief occupation. In the Finnmark fishing season, 7—10,000 vessels with 25,000 men practically live on the sea, and certainly make their living from it.

Apart from Norway proper, but placed under Norwegian sovereignty since 1920, lies the *Svalbard Archipelago* (Spitzbergen), comprising, with *Bjørnøya* (Bear Island) an area of about 25,000 sq.mi. The distance from the north of Norway to *South Cape* on Spitzbergen is 360 n. miles. With its enormous coal deposits, its marvellous Arctic scenery and bird life and its exceptionally pure air Svalbard is not only a great asset to Norway's economy, but also a tourist attraction of the first order.